new loyalties

Christian Faith and the Protestant Working Class

Philip Orr

For David

Warm Regards

Philip

"The neighbour is eternity's mark on every human being."

Søren Kierkegaard

CENTRE FOR CONTEMPORARY CHRISTIANITY IN IRELAND RESOURCE

introduction

This book is for anyone who genuinely cares about the fate of Ulster Protestant working-class communities in the 21st century. However, it will be of particular interest to those aspiring to manifest within these communities the gospel of Jesus Christ.

New Loyalties has been authored from within the Evangelical tradition and is therefore rooted in a reverence for Scripture and a respect for what the Protestant church holds as theological truth. However, I have also written the text in the conviction that the capacity for theological and biblical insight shrinks and dies when that church 'pulls up the drawbridge' and retreats behind its institutional walls, hiding away from the people with whom Christ himself would have most freely engaged. A process of mutual disengagement between much of the Protestant church and the working class seems to have begun during the Northern Ireland Troubles – just as the working-class communities were beginning to be hit by economic downturn, lawlessness, political disempowerment and social deprivation, with all the personal despair and ill-health that can follow in their wake. It is my belief that as a result of this disengagement, many churches have been sorely limited both in their insights and in their practice.

Perceptive Christians often recognise this limitation but may not know quite what to do about it. Such Christians might feel that their church needs to re-learn the arguments from Scripture about caring for those in need – from Our Lord's parable of the Good Samaritan to the call for social justice in the Old Testament prophets. They might want to back this up with a roll-call of all those theologians and Christian luminaries who, through the ages, have seen the need for both a social and an evangelistic gospel. However, it is my belief that this kind of 'head-knowledge' can only be put to good effect when making an open-minded journey of discovery, deep within Protestant working-class culture itself.

A good place to begin the journey is by examining the stark human need which exists in numerous Loyalist housing estates and on so many terraced streets where working-class Protestants live. It is then essential to face up to the dark gulf that has opened up between working-class culture and the many well-meaning people who belong to the church of Christ but who no longer possess a real connection to Loyalist communities. Equally challenging is the task of listening keenly to those adventurous Christians who have been trying to cross that gulf, sometimes at great personal cost. I believe it is only in the context of this three-part journey of discovery that relevant theological reflection can be undertaken – in which Scripture, spiritual tradition and the purpose and practice of the local church are all re-read in the light of what has been happening 'on the ground' in the very society in which we live. This short book invites you to embark on the journey described above and to pause and reflect from within your own experience as the route unfolds.

Chapter One outlines the social and economic malaise which exists in many working-class Loyalist communities – a complex problem, often mixed with a sense of political powerlessness and cultural abandonment. The Christian church understands very well that the personal regeneration brought by a personal faith in Christ will bring new hope and vitality to an individual life which has been darkened by what the Bible calls 'sin.' But how does the church help bring social regeneration to a whole community that has fallen on hard times? Does God even care about the social welfare of communities as well as the spiritual condition of individuals? And, if this is so, where in the Bible can we find political powerlessness and cultural abandonment being addressed with a message of hope? How do our biblical insights transfer into Christian practice?

In Chapter Two it will become clear that for many working-class people the perception that the church is a middle-class institution has given them cause to abandon it. The reader must ask if the church to which he or she belongs is middle-class in its values. Perhaps more crucially, does that church assume that these middle-class mores have scriptural justification? What features of that church's liturgy or its social activities would needlessly alienate a working-class person but not a middle-class member? Does Scripture have anything to say about creating a robust, positive relationship between the different social, cultural and economic groups that inevitably exist within a society? If so, then in what ways should the church attempt to straddle such differences within its own community life?

Chapter Three explores the nature of the Ulster Loyalist tradition. Much of the progressive Evangelical teaching of the last two decades has sought to guide the Protestant believer in Ireland away from an identification of faith with political ideology. But has this led to a 'holier-than-thou' approach to Loyalism, in which the church has turned its back on the cherished cultural values of a beleaguered community, in its search for an 'unaligned' ecclesiastical purity? Can the church perhaps offer a new and more positive role as a valued 'critical friend' of Loyalism? If so, do the Old Testament prophets sound like good role-models as ancient Israel's 'critical friends'? And what scriptural principles apply when faced with the violence committed in the past by Loyalist activists? Where exactly do restorative gestures of mercy towards 'ex-combatants' merge into tolerance or endorsement of wrong?

Chapter Four focuses on Billy Mitchell and his journey from Ulster Volunteer Force prisoner to Christian activist and thinker. Billy insisted throughout his writings that structural injustices in society are just as much a form of sin as the moral failings of the individual. Does this square theologically with the 'Reformed' tradition to which so many Ulster Protestants subscribe? Does it fit with the picture of Christ that we are given in the four Gospels and the teachings given in the apostolic letters? If a particular structural injustice does exist and it can be classified as sinful, then how should the church go about exposing it? Or better still, is the church able to model a better and more just way of conducting human affairs than the one it is critiquing?

Chapter Five offers , among other things, a survey of Christian community work in a couple of contexts outside Northern Ireland. One location is the city of Atlanta, Georgia, in the USA, where the work of Bob Lupton majors on what he calls 're-neighbouring'. This is the process whereby people of faith move in to 'problem areas' to share not just their Christian faith but also their skills, talents and their outlook on life with those new neighbours. Is there a 'theology of the neighbour' to be discerned in Scripture and in the teachings of the great Christian thinkers? Does it perhaps mean re-reading some overly-familiar Bible stories in new ways?

In the final chapter, I have tried to capture the thinking and practice of a range of leaders, activists and organisations whose purpose has been to 're-model' Christian ministry inside a Protestant working-class or Loyalist context. These ministries vary greatly in outlook, context and effect. I trust that readers will be inspired by the hard, creative and imaginative work being done, sometimes far from the centre of any denomination or ecclesiastical institution. Where readers disagree with the kinds of outreach being described, they may find it useful to ask on what grounds they disagree and what kind of alternative strategy they might propose for engagement.

Readers may dispute the validity of the facts, interpretations and opinions expressed by the author of this text. I trust that my factual errors have been kept to a minimum and that my interpretations have not been too wide of the mark. Where the opinions of the writer provoke radical disagreement, I trust that such discord may at least help readers to sharpen their own thinking and spur them on a path of their own choice which leads towards a society where spiritual and physical well-being are more widespread than they are today.

Philip Orr
April 2008

1

a community in need

The first section of this book examines the deprivation which characterises many working-class Protestant and Loyalist areas of Northern Ireland, using information from official reports, community audits and relevant census statistics. The chapter has also drawn on a number of interviews with professionals who work in these communities.

If a comparison is made with the far-off past, health and well-being are now widespread. In Belfast in 1895, life expectancy was in the mid 40s whereas by the end of the 20th century, most people could hope to live into their 70s. Moreover, in 1901, there were over 150 deaths per 1000 live births in the city whereas by 1999 that figure had dropped to six in every 1,000.[1] However, the reality remains that sizeable areas of Northern Ireland possess much poorer health, wealth, educational achievement and social opportunity than the rest of the population. The sectors of Northern Irish society labelled 'Protestant working class' are among the ones which suffer most.

The words 'Protestant working class' denote a diverse group. Not all working-class Protestants are Loyalists and not all Loyalists are working class. Nor should it be assumed that all working-class Protestants are unhealthy and impoverished or that all of them feel socially marginalised. Furthermore, what looks like dysfunction or impoverishment to naïve middle-class eyes may not be thought of as such by someone within a working-class context. Bad health, poverty and unhappiness may be found among middle-class people too, although they are usually in a much better position to access help in order to deal with their problems.

Deprived Loyalist Areas in Belfast

The Department for Social Development's (DSD) Task Force survey, called Renewing Communities, looked at disadvantage and distress in Loyalist working-class areas. It reported in 2004 and focused its attention largely on zones within inner-city Belfast, such as Sandy Row, Shankill and The Village. The report diagnosed, 'low educational achievement, low aspirations, physical and mental problems and apparent acceptance of economic inactivity.' It drew attention to 'fragmentation within the community', a situation exacerbated by paramilitary feuds. It pointed to an absence of strong, benign and effective local leadership.

The report also paid attention to the lack of academic or vocational qualifications, noting that from a very early age the local children seem predisposed to fail at education 'By the time they get to primary school, many pupils have already established poor behaviour patterns and demonstrate a low level capacity to engage positively with purposeful and structured learning.' The report's authors also noted unwillingness in these areas to avail of employment and to access opportunities for the skill enhancement and further education that might improve job prospects.

A range of statistics was used to indicate the severity of community impoverishment, using information from the 2001 Census and the so-called 'Noble Indicators' of multiple disadvantage. These indicators, which employ a blend of statistics, cover factors such as the levels of long-term sickness and the number of people who possess no educational qualifications. The report mentioned that of the 15 local government wards with the lowest proportion of school-leavers obtaining any school qualification, 13 were dominantly Protestant working class.

In the year in which the DSD survey was undertaken, throughout Northern Ireland as a whole, 39% of those who attempted the Eleven Plus transfer test – which measures academic attainment in upper primary-school children – obtained an A grade. Only 8% gained an A grade when taking the test in the Shankill district. This compared unfavourably with the 32% who obtained an A in adjacent Catholic West Belfast. In Northern Ireland as a whole, 35% of children opted out of taking the test, through no hope of obtaining a reasonable grade, while the figure was 67% in the Shankill area. The sense of disadvantage when compared to Catholic and Nationalist districts was compounded by the fact that only 13% of Shankill school children in this particular year went on to a grammar school – with its ready-made route towards higher education – whereas in the strongly working-class area of Catholic West Belfast, the corresponding figure was 21%.[2]

More recent figures produced in a report in The Irish News seem to confirm the relative weakness of working-class Protestant educational achievement. The report lists the 50 secondary (non-grammar) schools that achieved the best results at GCSE – these being the schools likely to have a considerable working-class intake. Only 18 were the 'state secondaries' whose pupils are predominantly Protestant. In the 'top 20' schools on this list of excellence, only four were within this 'state secondary' category. [3]

These findings resonate with the results of the Department of Social Development's report, suggesting high levels of incapacity for work within the modern, knowledge-based economy in Belfast's Loyalist areas. In the DSD survey, reference is made to the fact that in Crumlin, Shankill and Woodvale wards, all of which are strongly Protestant, the proportion of adults aged 25-74 with no educational qualifications amounted to 82%, 79% and 74% respectively.

The DSD report concerned itself not just with lack of education and skills but other features of disadvantage and discontent, painting a bleak picture of the Loyalist working class throughout Northern Ireland. It argued that this was a community which often seems without a sense of purpose, lacks an agreed local leadership, contains a highly disaffected 'underclass' and often struggles with the tense and demoralising 'interface' problems that manifest themselves where Loyalist and Nationalist areas meet.

This is a community that also contends with high levels of paramilitary intimidation and in smaller rural and border areas feels isolated and too insignificant demographically to achieve substantive political representation. The survey suggested that contraction of security force-related employment due to the 'closure' of the Troubles has often hit Protestant communities hard, as has the disappearance over the last few decades of heavy industry. Population shifts, involving the movement of the 'brightest and best' to housing in the suburbs or in fine rural locations, has left many Loyalist working-class areas feeling stranded, without talent and hope. The dismay at the perceived political and cultural successes of Nationalist working-class communities – who now have representatives in high government office – is also palpable.

All these factors have resulted in communities often too demoralised and disorganised to present bids for funding for renewal of their own neighbourhoods. The report argued that the grip of paramilitary organisations prevents the impulse for renewal from gaining momentum, noting their intense territorial control and describing their overall impact as being deeply negative because they have, 'imposed a self-interest agenda… denied communities opportunities to participate and develop and have enticed young people into illegal activities…' The report also noted the prevalence in these working-class areas of alcohol and drug abuse, of obesity, lack of exercise and poor diet. It also focused on issues of stress, depression, self-harm and suicide.

There were also alarming teenage pregnancy figures in Sandy Row and The Village, where in 2001, 13% and 15% respectively of all pregnancies were among girls under 16. Both figures were well above the Eastern Health and Social Services Board average of 8%. In the context of poor economic opportunity and social stress, early pregnancy augurs badly for the prospects of both mother and child. Another negative factor which can be added to the mix is the low priority often given to affordable social housing in the recent context of market-led property development and house-price inflation, leading many working-class people to feel they will not be able to afford a future in their area.

Yet the report did not ignore the good work already being done by a range of statutory, voluntary and faith-based bodies to tackle some of these problems. It also suggested that there is a role in troubled communities for the church, which is 'in on the ground', possesses a reservoir of volunteer energy and is usually committed 'for the long haul'. It recommended that faith-based and voluntary bodies should partner with the statutory sector to seek a range of funding from across all government departments in order to bring greater levels of care, empowerment and support to needy inhabitants of places such as Sandy Row, Shankill and The Village.[4]

Loyalist Deprivation Across Northern Ireland

It is helpful to look more closely at some of the statistics from the 2001 Census for the working class in the local government ward of Shankill in Protestant West Belfast and the figures from Malone, a prosperous ward of mixed religion in South Belfast.

In 2001, the Shankill ward had a total population of 3,784, of which only 24 declared themselves to be Roman Catholic, rendering it a culturally homogeneous area. In Malone, out of a population of 5,694 there were 2,881 Catholics, rendering it a 'mixed' area. Within the Shankill ward there was a high incidence of one-person households, with 451 lone-parent households and 467 one-person pensioner households. In Malone, which possesses a greater population, there were only 112 lone-parent households and just 295 one-person pensioner dwellings. In the Shankill area, 1,821 people between the ages of 16 and 74 possessed no qualifications and 1,347 people in the area – no less than 36% – were suffering from some kind of limiting, long-term illness. In Malone only 441 16-74 year olds had no qualifications and the number of people suffering from a limiting, long-term illness was 690 – a mere 12% of the population.

These figures confirm the findings mentioned above. Compared with other parts of the city which are situated only a few miles away, the Shankill is in a state of deprivation. Relatively speaking, levels of illness are high, levels of prosperity are low and levels of educational attainment are meagre. Many inhabitants have to face the challenges of living alone or of bringing up children without the economic and emotional aid of a resident spouse.[5]

However, problems are not confined to the inner city, as an examination of some of the 36 zones designated as Neighbourhood Renewal Areas under the government's recent 'People and Place' strategy for tackling deprivation reveals. Contrasts similar to those between Shankill and Malone exist within much smaller, predominantly Protestant towns such as Carrickfergus in County Antrim.

In the town's working class Sunnylands estate, 31% of the population has a limiting, long-term illness compared with 19% in Carrickfergus as a whole. In the Sunnylands ward in 2005, just 25% of the area's GCSE students gained five or more 'good' grades whereas the figure for Carrickfergus as a whole was 65%. Out of the 1,377 enrolments within the town in higher education during this period, only 17 were from Sunnylands. In Sunnylands only 54% of the people had access to a car or a van, whereas in the nearby Victoria ward 79% had this kind of access. A poor public transport infrastructure means lack of access to a vehicle can be a real handicap. Working-class disadvantage is thus a feature of Carrickfergus, even though it is not a place where morale is adversely affected by 'interface' issues or by tensions concerning the routing of local Loyalist parades.

There are other 'poor' areas in towns such as Ballyclare, Newtownards and Ballymena where to the casual observer considerable prosperity and well-being appears to be the order of the day. One Neighbourhood Renewal Area, within Ballyclare in County Antrim, contains a population of 957, of whom 92% are Protestant. Almost 30% of the population suffer a limiting, long-term illness. Given that only 40% of the people have access to a car or van, serious and costly transportation problems are posed by the fact that the nearest Post Office is 1.64km away for the average inhabitant and the nearest hospital 11.74km. The problem must be particularly acute for the 29% of the area's households that are occupied by lone pensioners, or the 11% occupied by lone-parent families.

In the Bangor Renewal Area, which includes the large Kilcooley estate, similar problems with health, skills and mobility are found. Almost 54% of the inhabitants do not possess any qualifications. The number without qualifications grows in the upper end of the age profile. Seventy-five percent of 45-59 year olds have no qualifications and 90% of 60-74 year olds are in a similar position. This makes it almost impossible for most older citizens to gain useful, skilled employment and must endanger financial security, lower self-esteem and narrow aspirations within an important section of the population.

In Ballymena's Renewal Area a similar pattern emerges. There is a 16% figure for lone parent households, compared to the Northern Ireland average of 8%. Over 47% of the population have no access to a car or a van. Fifty-nine percent of the residents live in some form of rented accommodation, a housing category which need not be a sign of severe deprivation but may nonetheless indicate low income and limited social mobility. A total of 59% possess no qualifications and that figure rises to 76% amongst 45-59 year olds and 92% amongst 60-74 year olds.[6]

Health Problems and the Fragmentation of Community

Research on the subject of working-class alienation was undertaken in 2003 for the Office of the First Minister and Deputy First Minister. This report is careful to point out that Catholic working-class areas also suffer from intense levels of impoverishment and that it is quite wrong to assume that Nationalist communities always have a high level of positive collectivist values. The report stresses that low morale

too often characterises both Protestant and Catholic housing estates, noting the 'high levels of apathy that prevail' and observing a culture of 'low expectations' and 'disengagement'. The authors of the report concur with the DSD report that too often these estates have been 'dominated by paramilitary organisations and terrorists turned gangsters.'

The researchers agree with the DSD report that community organisation was often seriously under-developed in Protestant areas. They suggest that there has been a reluctance to seek help in tackling deprivation, given that Protestants have been tied to loyalty to the state, rather than tackling the state for its failures. This is given as a good reason why there has been less likelihood of Loyalist groups presenting applications for funding for community intervention. A number of community activists interviewed by the authors of this report gave illuminating responses. One interviewee said:

'The Protestant ethos is that community stuff is like charity, is like handouts and that it somehow is a slur on their working ethos. And they don't ever require that help…Protestant people are their own worst enemy when it comes to development because of the psyche that they have, the individualism …showing weakness would have meant that the Northern Ireland state wasn't working. It would have been to say "the state has failed" and that would have given credence to our enemies…'

Another respondent also spoke of a 'big fragmentation' in Protestant areas: 'We don't come together very well at all; we all work separately at our own issues. We don't see the big picture at all. If one group gets funding they won't let the other groups know where they got it from…'[7]

The results yielded by studies of Ulster Protestant deprivation in 2003 and 2004 would be no surprise to anyone familiar with the survey of public health in the Greater Shankill area conducted in the mid 1990s.[8] This report, undertaken before the worst Loyalist feuding greatly exacerbated the state of mental health in the area, nonetheless painted a grim enough picture.

The report looked at issues related to personal well-being such as education and wages. It noted the fact that 83% of the area's residents possessed no qualifications, that only one in every 12 children from Shankill managed to gain entry to a grammar school and that only 1% of the area's residents were educated to degree level. When these statistics are taken in tandem with the poor figures for education in the DSD report for 2004, there is little evidence of social improvement over the intervening years.

This survey went on to observe that 34% of males and 56% of females were economically inactive. This helps explain the statistic that whereas the average disposable income in Ulster at this time was £235, the average on the Shankill Road was less than £100. As a result, 78% of local householders received some kind of social security benefit and 30% of all households depended regularly on money borrowed midweek in order to 'get by'.

The survey showed that 42% of the area's population was classified by the medical authorities as having a 'health problem', with 11% of all adults receiving help with a 'mental health' issue. No less than 25% of all women in the area had taken medication for 'mental health problems'. The fact that 10% of all Shankill parents believed their children of primary-school age to be smoking throws light on the statistic that 15% of all young people in the area were suffering from some kind of chest illness. Fifty-one percent of all young people in the mid to older-teen age-range were drinking alcohol on a regular basis, thereby storing up future health problems as well as creating much greater likelihood of the sort of anti-social behaviour which demoralises a neighbourhood.

The incidence of lone parenthood on The Shankill was found to be high, a fact later borne out by the 2001 Census. Thirty-nine percent of all families with dependents under the age of 16 were being parented alone. The realities of financial hardship and the perils of unhealthy lifestyles for these mothers were clear: 85% of these lone parents had an income of less than £100 a week, 69% had to borrow money mid-week and 65% smoked on a regular basis. The other sizeable group of residents who lived alone consisted of the elderly. Twenty-five percent of households fell into that category and the isolation felt by many was reflected in the fact that 17% of all lone, elderly citizens were suffering from clinical depression.

A later report, undertaken by the local 'Shankill 21' focus group in 2002, indicated another key feature of this Loyalist community, its sense of disaffiliation from a police service that seems inaccessible and alien at times of crisis. The report's author commented 'working-class Loyalists are disenfranchised, resulting in police being regarded as a foreign body, not belonging to the local community – the procedure for accessing the police service is not widely understood and this can lead to problems and dissatisfaction.' The 'disenfranchisement' mentioned here is connected to a local sense that both the educational qualifications needed and the recent 'bias' towards the recruitment of Catholics – motivated by a governmental desire to create a 'cross-community' force – have made it much too hard for working-class Protestants to gain employment as police officers.[9]

The plight of various groups within Loyalist communities is obvious. The situation of many young mothers is evident in the statistics cited above, as are the dangers faced by Loyalist young people in a world where drugs and alcohol are easily available, where casual street violence is all too rife and where family ties and moral boundaries have been greatly loosened. This at-risk group is dealt with at length by one interviewee in the final chapter of this publication.

The experience of the elderly, often having to cope with meagre resources, is reflected in a survey of the attitudes of senior citizens, published by the LINC Resource Centre in North Belfast, in 2007.

'We've lost the sense of community. We would have helped one another, now it's all closed doors. You live beside ones and don't know their name; there is more money about now but we used to be dependent on one another... now people just look after themselves, mind their own business; back then you kept an eye on your neighbour... you are more isolated because you keep your door locked and be wary opening it...morals have dissolved during the Troubles (which) were a big influence on how communities evolved... law and order disappeared... respect is gone.'

One senior citizen dwelt on the difficulties of living near an 'interface' and offered his opinion on the role of the police:

'Nobody likes the peace line but it is a necessary evil...where I live now is right on an interface and even with the peace line there are still attacks from both sides over it, petrol bombs and all sorts. When you ask the peelers, all they say is that, "we have a patrol car in the area." What good is that if the petrol bombs are still coming in?'[10]

Protestants as a Minority Community

For some Protestant communities, the sense of being at a disadvantage is particularly potent because they exist in an area dominated by Catholics and Nationalists. This can be particularly true west of the River Bann where Republicanism is a dominant political force. A study of the dilemmas faced by the minority Protestant community in and around Maghera in County Londonderry, may be found in the last chapter.

Particularly rural forms of deprivation come into play for some Ulster Protestants – ones that are not acknowledged by the Noble Indicators. These include the magnified sense of isolation for poor rural families who cannot afford a car and who suffer from meagre or non-existent public transport facilities. There is also the fact that many rural houses stand much more exposed to wintry and damp weather than do city dwellings – a fact that is not acknowledged by any rural fuel grant.

One area where Protestants feel themselves to be a troubled minority is in the city of Derry. The Protestant population of the Cityside area, west of the River Foyle, shrank by over 83% between 1971 and 1991. Even in the Waterside area, east of the river, where Protestants have traditionally felt safer, the Catholic population has risen by over 21%, which has created a sense of relative Protestant decline even though their own numbers have remained reasonably stable.

A survey undertaken in 2003 by a team from Queen's University Belfast and the University of Ulster found that 80% of Derry Protestants felt their community to be in political decline and 74% agreed with the statement, 'My cultural tradition is always the underdog.' No less than 65% of all Protestant respondents believed that the 'other' community wanted their community to 'move out of the city', while only 4% agreed that the Protestant community now felt strong enough to move back into the Cityside. Forty percent of the interviewees felt that their own community members were discriminated against when seeking work and 80% stated that they would feel too scared to walk through a Catholic area after dark. Typical comments included the following:

'I go to Coleraine or Limavady... even small things like if there was a bakery and the one in the Waterside doesn't have it you go to the one in Eglinton. I have this thing now that its theirs [Cityside] and let them keep it, I wouldn't support them... If you go over the town now you'll see tricolours will be flying... you'll see people walking about... with Glasgow Celtic shirts... and that's to say, "I am a Catholic, you're not wanted here." It's a subtle form of intimidation.'

There is a sense that the Waterside area is being deliberately under resourced 'We are 20 years behind the Cityside when it comes to development. Derry City Council have been over funding the Cityside this last 15 years...' And there is bitterness about the unwelcoming nature of the City Cemetery where Republican flags, plaques and statues are highly visible, 'There are people buried up there whose wife and husband are still living and when their time comes will not be buried up in that City Cemetery – they'll be buried in

the Waterside where their relatives can visit them in a bit of peace.'

Among the other sources of concern were bus stops for transport to Protestant areas of the city, which were said to be regular targets of Catholic abuse. Protestant school children, wearing school blazers on the city side of the river, were also said to be victims of harassment. The writers of this report concluded by diagnosing a number of dangers for the Protestants of Derry which mirror findings already cited in this chapter, including fragmentation and rivalry within the community due to paramilitary feuds, a relative lack of community-development skills and a failure to network with the relevant statutory agencies. The writers also pointed out the danger of younger, well-employed, more mobile inhabitants of the Protestant community moving out of Derry, leaving behind an older, more benefit-dependant and more vulnerable population. Undoubtedly what holds true for Derry holds true for many other Protestant areas of Northern Ireland where the regular issues of poverty and social decline are augmented by a sense of being a victimised cultural minority.[11]

In Derry's Waterside area, community activist and former Loyalist miliant, Glenn Barr, offered thoughts about the Loyalist community in his vicinity. They echo the findings described above. He suggested that the community was 'in a pretty bad shape', that it was 'leaderless …uninterested in voting and subject to the drink culture.' He feels that Protestants 'know little or nothing about their own culture and history' and that 'too many are just anti-nationalist rather than knowing what it is that they should stand for.' He describes how 'those who were able to leave the Waterside for the North Antrim Coast, at first for the weekend then, many of them, to settle there…' The 'left behinds' have a resultant sense of low morale.

Barr has attempted to tackle this issue of low morale by promoting pride in local culture and to that end the Waterside Theatre was created, to offer young people in particular the chance to debate and perform. It is now a centre of excellence for music but, according to Barr, sadly, not too many of the local working-class children are among those who use it. Barr also noted that the theatre has a very good annual pantomime and that they can fill the hall many times over with 'Catholic audiences', coming from as far away as Letterkenny across the border in the Republic. However he claimed that the local 'state schools', containing Waterside's Protestant children, have been reluctant to send their students. He wondered if it was because a class-conscious Protestant educational establishment shies away from him and his theatre because of the associations with his advocacy of working-class Loyalism and his militant past?[12]

Community Problems Observed at First Hand

Others who work within Loyalist and Protestant working-class communities are able to observe on a daily basis the problems that have been described in this chapter. One Protestant minister[13] whose work is located within a Belfast inner-city area speaks, much as Glenn Barr does, of low morale that affects his people, leading them to the opinion that 'the glass is always half-empty rather than half-full'. He mentions a local primary school where only a couple of the 40 children of transfer-test age were actually deemed able enough to sit the exam in a recent year. He speaks of the way in which the numerous churches in the area still tend to compete with one another for 'clients', rather than working together, despite the fact that the population of the area has gone down markedly in recent times. He believes that the influence of the Ulster Defence Association in recent years has been a factor leading to fear and reluctance to speak out or participate in community affairs.

Despite all this, his church has endeavoured to reach out in novel ways, setting up a 'prayer table' in the car park of a local supermarket where requests for prayer may be handed in. This particular minister feels that one of the key factors alienating many local Protestant working-class people from the church is the feeling that when the Troubles came along, the church retreated, with many of its members moving to the suburbs and returning only on Sunday in their shiny cars, to worship for an hour then drive away again. It is a complaint that we will see repeated elsewhere in this text.

Ironically, the economic prudence and personal aspiration which often attend a Christian lifestyle can carry problems for working-class communities. Committed Christians are likely to work hard, achieve promotion or seek new job opportunities with better wages and save their earnings, thus affording more comfortable homes in 'better' locations, where they can bring up their children in a 'better' environment. This process of faith-inspired mobility is often spoken of as 'redemption lift' and it can drain a working-class area of 'people of faith' who might be its most valuable asset. Their only remaining contact with their community of origin may be attending their 'home church' on Sunday morning or visiting aged relatives on an irregular basis.

Another interviewee[14] works in an educational scheme located in a working-class Loyalist estate in County Down, run under the auspices of a well-known charity and specialising in pre-school care for mothers and children, enabling the youngsters to come to their first year at primary school with an improved ability to make use of education. The estate in which she works constitutes one of the most disadvantaged local government wards in Northern Ireland, measured in terms of multiple levels of deprivation. She describes it as a classic area of low aspiration and, while it would be very wrong to suggest that poor parenting is a universal feature of the area, nonetheless, many of the young mothers whom she encounters possess neither qualifications nor jobs, suffer from low self-esteem and are thereby in danger of passing on such things to their children.

Among these young women exists what she calls a 'pyjama culture' where, having taken their children to school clad in pyjamas, dressing gown and slippers, they return to bed to watch daytime television with few or no activities planned for the day ahead. Many of them are single mothers while others have stories, which they may do their best to hide, of domestic violence initiated by a difficult husband. All of them suffer from the fact that the estate is in the 'middle of nowhere'. Amenities are poor and many families are without a car, which means paying for taxi fares in order to visit the supermarket or some other facility. A culture of negativity and a sense of deprivation is handed down through the generations.

It is in this negative context she believes the work of her scheme is crucial. Many children have arrived at the local primary school without a basic curiosity about the world around them, without an elementary linguistic framework and with an impoverished capacity for play. It is clear that many young mothers in the estate – early parenting is mainly done by the mothers – have no idea of how to engage in play with their toddlers and don't tend to nurture their capacity for language. Instead a dummy is put in the child's mouth and it is placed in front of a TV or video screen. As a result, that child arrives into school lacking the experience of 'educational play', of simple dialogue and of the joys of discovery.

There are also serious dietary issues to be confronted among these parents and their children. 'Healthy eating' drives are a regular feature of the program in order to tackle sugar and fat addictions, to advise young mothers against filling baby bottles with 'sweetie drinks' and to ask them to cut down on feeding their children confectionery, which is largely responsible for an epidemic of children's tooth decay in the area.

However, the main job for the project is to provide a friendly, creative crèche environment where pre-school children can be encouraged to participate in stimulating play and asked to listen to stories or engage in early linguistic activity. The workers endeavour to operate with mothers and children together, teaching young women to interact more fully and positively with their offspring.

In the case of some parents who are too lacking in self-esteem to make an appearance at the nursery premises, a family support visitor will have been asked by the local health visitor to make a call, bringing a range of educational toys, which the mother is encouraged to employ. Eventually the young woman in question is encouraged to leave the 'safety' of the house and attend the nursery. Also significant is the provision of support to families once their children have started school, particularly by means of homework clubs. In addition, the provision of opportunities to learn the basics in Maths, English, Computers and Cookery is of great importance in raising self-confidence of young mothers within the estate. An NVQ qualification can be gained and this can add immensely to the self-belief of the person who has worked hard and gained a tangible reward.

Ulster's middle-class culture is not without its own distinct problems. This chapter does not suggest that working-class Protestant people need reshaped as upwardly-mobile, home-owning professionals. An aspiration to be middle-class is not an appropriate answer to the 'poverty of aspiration' found in many working-class environments.

However, it is clear that deprivation in Protestant working-class communities is an endemic and painful phenomenon and that this deprivation is about more than lack of money. Failure to flourish in Sandy Row or the Waterside or on a Ballymena council estate may have to do with a radical lack of political hope, a bleak domestic or civic environment or lack of support during an unhealed illness. There may be a dearth of useful personal skills for living in a complex modern age, an absence of creative local leadership or lack of agreed structures for community support. It may be about crime. It may be about total disillusionment with politics and politicians. It may also be about the lack of spiritual purpose and a sustaining community of faith. However, the primary economic hardship for many, of low-paid work or a life spent on benefits, should not be underestimated.

The governmental reports, local surveys and census data examined in this chapter offer proof of the deep-seated problems described in the interviews with those who engage in community work in Loyalist areas. This evidence makes it obvious that problems exist in a variety of geographical locations, not just in highly visible parts of inner-city Belfast.

The next chapter will investigate whether Northern Ireland's Protestant churches are rising to the challenge of helping to change the situation.

[1] Figures are taken from Alun Evans, 'Health in Belfast' in *Enduring City: Belfast in the Twentieth Century*, eds. F.W. Boal and S.A. Royle (Blackstaff Press, 2006).

[2] Statistical information used here is carried in the publications section of the Department of Social Development website www.dsdni.gov.uk/40708_action_plan.pdf and www.dsdni.gov.uk/40708_task_force.pdf. Accessed 5 May 2007.

[3] The Irish News, 3 May 2007.

[4] See www.dsdni.gov.uk/40708_task_force.pdf and www.dsdni.gov.uk/40708_action_plan.pdf. Accessed 7 May 2007.

[5] Statistical information on the 2001 Census is located at www.nisra.gov.uk. Accessed 9 May 2007.

[6] Statistical information on 2001 Census figures and, in particular, on neighbourhood renewal areas is at www.nisra.gov.uk. Accessed 10 May 2007

[7] See the report by Ed Cairns et al entitled *Social Capital, Collectivism-Individualism and Community Background in Northern Ireland* on the website of the Office of First Minister and Deputy First Minister of Northern Ireland www.ofmdfmni.gov.uk/social-capital.pdf. Accessed 13 May 2007.

[8] 'A Health Profile of the Greater Shankill Area, Making Belfast Work', *Community Development Journal*, Volume 33, Number 3, pp 205-225. © 1998 Community Development Journal and Oxford University Press.

[9] *Greater Shankill 21 Report and Action Plan*, (Health Action Zone, May 2002) p 16.

[10] *A Senior Citizens' Role in Peace Building*, (LINC Resource Centre, May 2007) pp 21-31.

[11] Peter Shirlow et al, *Population Change and Social Inclusion Study* Derry/Londonderry 2005, (St Columb's Park House, Derry, 2006) pp 2-18.

[12] Interview with Glenn Barr, Derry, November 2007.

[13] The minister referred to here was interviewed in Belfast under conditions of anonymity.

[14] The child-care worker referred to here was interviewed in Belfast under conditions of anonymity.

2

a church in retreat?

The relationship between Loyalist working-class communities and the Protestantism to which they still claim theoretical allegiance, was once much closer than it is today. This is partly because of the secularisation which has taken place here, as it has everywhere in Western Europe. However, other key factors are specific to the recent history of Northern Ireland. This chapter will uncover the spirit of Protestant community engagement that once existed, look at factors which led to its decline and illustrate how the church's capacity to deal with social need has thus been limited. However, new opportunities for social engagement will also be suggested.

The Long Tradition of Church Engagement with Need

The Shankill area of Belfast has had a long history of working-class poverty. It has also had a spiritual tradition of vibrant Evangelicalism coupled with confident social involvement. The famous Shankill Road Mission, founded in 1898 by the Presbyterian Church in Ireland, pioneered social care throughout the first half of the 20th century as well as 'proclaiming the gospel'. This care included free medical treatment for those who could not afford it and free holidays for those who would never otherwise leave their area.

The Mission founded a 'Fresh Air Colony' and a 'Holiday Home of Rest' in Bangor, County Down. Now in the first decade of the 21st century, almost everyone on the Shankill Road of advanced years can recall the holidays offered widely in the area in the years before the Second World War, when, for a week, children from homes where life was tough and money was scarce could enjoy hearty meals, a comfortable bed and a variety of games and leisure activities, including regular visits to the beach. A copy of the newspaper, *The Missionary Herald*, for October 1939, reported how in the summer of that year the mission had 'provided over 1,700 of the neediest children we could find with at least one week's free holiday.' In addition, the paper mentioned how '748 mothers and children were entertained, at very modest cost to themselves'. The story focused on how 'in many cases the children require to be suitably clothed by the mission before they can be taken.' Also in the summer of 1939 the 'Poor Children's Annual Day of Delight' provided a free day-trip to Donaghadee for over 800 boys and girls.

However, the Mission's activities were certainly not confined to the summer, as the same edition of the newspaper indicated 'Every week cases of extreme need and hardship are dealt with and helped with groceries, clothing, sickness supplies and fuel. At the Christmas season, the mission has been able to send into over 2,000 homes annually, a substantial parcel of food and good cheer, with special delicacies for the aged and sick…'[1]

The Shankill area in the mid 20th century had been a community of over 50,000 people, sustaining almost 50 places of worship, including numerous small independent mission halls.[2] Most of them energetically pursued the task of caring for local people. One such body was the Campbell Street Mission in an area of the Shankill that was flattened in the interests of 'redevelopment' in the mid-1960s. Even up to the days of its demise, this little faith-based group catered for social need. Its magazine for the autumn of 1964 mentioned the hall's 'annual outing to the seaside for poor children and old folk' and its seasonal gifts to homes 'where unemployment and sickness have so lowered incomes that the children who live there will have a cheerless Christmas.' Gifts also went out to homes belonging to 'old folk whose meagre pensions do not allow any of those little treats such as a really good fire or something nice to eat.'

The editor of the magazine also took due note of the fact that even in the 1960s 'some of the houses' in the area consisted of 'one room or at the most two rooms' and contained 'families numbering 8 or 10'. The writer reminded readers, 'It is grand to think that our Lord visited the homes of the sick and the dying' and encouraged them to 'follow his example', quoting a poem that spoke of Christ's love incarnated in the good deeds of the believer:

Not I but Christ to gently soothe in sorrow,
Not I but Christ to wipe the falling tear,
Not I but Christ to lift the heavy burden,
Not I but Christ to hush away all fear.

In the last few years before it was demolished, the Campbell Street Mission also had thriving youth clubs, including a boys' group that provided courses for the young lads of the district in 'model-making, simple electronics, photography and mechanical engineering.' The youth leaders who supervised these boys made sure that 'every opportunity is given for them to sit around and chat'. The girls' group had a membership of over 100 teenagers. Their activities included singing, drama and elocution, which would 'give the children that confidence which helps them to take their place in life.'

The Campbell Street Mission, according to its magazine, was there to minister to everyone and was motivated by the penury of many people in the district in which it was located, where it was still common in the 1960s to see 'old people with few clothes on them' and to witness 'children playing in the streets on a cold November day, wearing a thin summer frock. To find a lad in his teens going off to school with shoes that let water in and out at the same time. To visit a home and find that the main meal is tea, bread and butter or find the unemployed father washing and preparing the food for the family while mammy is in hospital.' Very often, Campbell Street's kindness to the poor even extended to ensuring that 'rent is paid and poverty-stricken homes are helped over a difficult place.' According to the magazine's editor, the church's motto was the instruction of Jesus, 'In as much as ye do it unto the least of these – ye do it unto me.'[3]

This example of very practical concern by an Evangelical mission hall in one part of Belfast was but a small part of a tradition of Irish church involvement with social issues. The Methodist Church in Ireland's history of care is a particularly rich one, going back to the 18th century. One of the first things Methodists did on arriving in Ireland was to raise money to release people trapped in debtors' gaols. They established almshouses for elderly women as early as the 1760s and a home for poverty-stricken ex-soldiers in the 1790s. They visited hospitals, prisons and convict ships and assisted with education and training for those who might benefit. In the 19th and early 20th centuries their orphan society raised money and their homes for orphaned children provided love and support for some of the country's most vulnerable children.[4]

Other mainstream Protestant denominations also worked hard at providing social care throughout the 19th and 20th centuries. A Presbyterian-based mission to the 'deaf and dumb' was founded in 1857 and a Presbyterian Orphan Society was created in 1866, which throughout the next 100 years would deal with no less than 35,000 unparented children. The church's Old Age Fund, founded in 1906, helped 1,000 elderly people during its first decade. The Belfast Town Mission, founded as early as 1827, had as its chief aim to promote the kingdom of God 'among the poor, the careless and the churchless.' Throughout Presbyterian history, hundreds of deaconesses were charged with the task of reaching out to young mothers struggling with the duties of family life in tough domestic circumstances.[5]

This outreach of the past was a product of different social conditions. The churches confidently coupled practical compassion with explicit evangelisation in a way that would meet opposition from many whose values are shaped by contemporary pluralism. These were also more paternalistic times. Generosity by Christians who possessed some wealth and means was happily accepted by those who suffered at the bottom of the social hierarchy due to the widespread physical poverty and an unassailable class structure. Nowadays vast inequalities still exist but grinding, wretched poverty is a rarer phenomenon. In any case, within recent times the state rather than the church has become the expected provider of help to those in need.

The Realities of Religious Decline

It may seem as if Protestant churches in Northern Ireland are still operating from a position of strength within their local communities. A recent Queen's University Belfast survey in the province indicates that out of the section of the population which calls itself Protestant, 34% still attend church once a week or more and that only 19% never attend. The figures for Ulster Catholics are also high and, as the survey's chief researcher, sociologist Claire Mitchell, has pointed out, Northern Ireland is therefore 'among the most religious societies in Western Europe and indeed the world.' She cites recent statistics which suggest that feeling oneself to be a part of Protestant culture is widespread, even among the young. Eighty-eight percent of Protestant 15-17 year olds say that they feel themselves to be part of their religious community and 59% state that their religion is important to them, even if this may be a badge of identity rather than a mark of spiritual convictions.[6] The figures for youth work are also impressive. They indicate an on-going relationship between churches and the younger generation. Research done in 2006 points to over two-thirds of registered youth groups and almost three-quarters of all youth workers in Northern Ireland being faith-based.[7]

However, in1968, on the eve of the Troubles, 46% Protestants attended church on a weekly basis as opposed to 34% in 2003.[8] One researcher, Ian McAlister, has noted that in the 2001 Census, nearly 14% of the population described themselves as having no religion, compared to just 2% in 1961. McAlister regards the secular group in Ulster society as the fourth largest after Catholics, Presbyterians and Anglicans and reckons that if the current trend continues, secularists will become the second or third largest group in Northern Ireland by the time of the next census in 2011.[9] The results of a recent survey on basic religious knowledge, carried out by the Evangelical Alliance in Northern Ireland, should also give cause for concern to church leaders. The findings, which were published in December 2007, indicated that only 36% of Protestants knew there were four Gospels, only 45% were able to name the Holy Trinity and just 26% could recall the First Commandment.[10]

Materialism and secularism feature as reasons for religious decline in Northern Ireland as they do elsewhere, making many churches in many countries feel that they are 'on the back foot' in promoting Christian values. However, of equal local significance for working-class religious culture here has been the violence of the Troubles which since 1969 has led to the demographic shift noted in the previous chapter. Many of those Protestant church members who could do so moved to the suburbs or comfortable country towns from working-class locations, leaving behind communities who were falling prey to paramilitary control and suffering the economic decline that attended the demise of the Ulster manufacturing industry.

In many areas of the province, both rural and urban, Protestant churches have lost their congregations as those who felt themselves to be a threatened minority in a Nationalist or 'interface' area have moved to 'safer ground'. Some churches have had to close. As the Presbyterian minister Norman Hamilton has noted, two Protestant churches in North Belfast closed on the same Sunday in August 1999.[11] Meanwhile, non-religious notions of intervention in Northern Ireland's social dilemmas became normative in wave after wave of government policy, focusing on a secular concept of 'community development' in which the disadvantaged are enabled to build 'social capital' through self-education, voluntary action, economic 'start-ups', 'grass-roots' initiatives and local leadership.

As the writer Derek Bacon has pointed out, 'Until the 1970s the religious world was stable. Church leadership was trained for a familiar task in a system undisturbed for generations. There was strength in this way and little call for experimentation or specialist ministries of the kind taken for granted elsewhere on these islands.' Bacon goes on to claim that several decades later 'with the traditional model no longer working as it once did and their central bodies under equipped to offer incisive support' many local churches are 'struggling to meet the demands of a world conditioned by realities they were unable or unwilling to foresee.'[12]

Church and the community: Ravenhill and Elsewhere

Several studies conducted in the last two decades confirm the widespread nature of the problems to which Bacon alludes. In 1995, the researcher Christine Acheson published the results of a survey undertaken in the Lower Ravenhill area of inner-city Belfast. She discovered five 'established' churches belonging to the main Protestant denominations and five congregations that might be classified either as mission halls or 'recently established' churches belonging to smaller denominations. Out of the 32 listed church leaders in these congregations, only three actually lived in the Lower Ravenhill area. Only 28% of 'church attenders' lived in the area, leaving 72% who 'came in from elsewhere' to worship on Sunday mornings. In fact, 31% of the Lower Ravenhill's churchgoers used to reside locally but had now moved out of the area. Amongst the church members who travelled into the city to worship were individuals who lived in locations as far afield as Bangor, Saintfield and Glengormley. Furthermore, in the ten churches studied by Acheson, only 1% of the members fell into the category of long-term unemployed compared with a truly devastating 30% of the population in the Lower Ravenhill area. Only 13% of the church members lived alone whereas the figure for the local area was 34%. Quite clearly the make up of the churches in this particular and often impoverished part of Belfast was not reflective of the social mix of the neighbourhood and showed considerable dependence, for both leadership and membership, on those who lived elsewhere.

Acheson undertook 42 personal interviews throughout the district, endeavouring to gain a balanced picture of attitudes to religion. Of her interviewees, only four went to a church or mission hall regularly. The perception of the residents was that church was not a key player in everyday adult life in the area, as 22 interviewees said that it was 'elderly people who go to church' and nine said that 'young children go.' Twenty-two interviewees said that 'a supermarket is the greatest need in the area' rather than expressing need in any religious form. When asked what churches or mission halls had to offer 20-40 year olds, people with disabilities, men, unemployed people and single parents, approximately two-thirds of the total responses said either 'I don't know' or 'nothing' to these questions, although 31 nonetheless expressed the vague opinion that they would like to see faith-based groups 'more involved in the local community'.

Acheson also talked to church and mission hall leaders. The impression she received was of a conservative perspective on interaction with the community, which was 'generally seen in terms of evangelism and outreach, with the aim of conversions and increased church attendance by local residents'. The opinion was widely held that 'local adults need to support churches and mission halls if they are to get any help'. They suggested that the relationship between people in need and the church must be 'two-way'. A clear division between 'spiritual' and 'social' issues was felt to be paramount with the former being of much greater importance. Evangelism and preaching were seen as the only really crucial tasks of the church in the Lower Ravenhill and that positive changes in the church's relationship with the community were more likely to come from 'spiritual awakening or Revival' rather than from making new attempts to bridge the social gulfs that might have opened up between church and community. There was also a widespread sense that in reaching out to deal with local need there was a real danger of 'being swamped, losing control and compromising the faith.'[13]

A few years previously, a series of conferences held in Belfast on the topic of community development in Protestant areas resulted in a forthright expression of opinions by community workers that make interesting reading in the light of Acheson's survey.[14] These discussions took place as long ago as 1991 but there has been little evidence of overall improvement in church/community relations since that date so it may be assumed that the views expressed still reflect some of the realities of the situation.

One commentator suggested that 'the churches have lost ground, especially in the inner city and there has been a general breakdown in the moral fibre of the community. Churches are out of touch with local people.' Another participant spoke of how 'the churches support a Protestant work ethic which alienates the unemployed'. Some speakers suggested that 'many community groups could never have a dialogue with those evangelical churches which focus on the other world and preach hell-fire and damnation, doing little or nothing to improve conditions in this world.' It was also stated that churches which do get involved in community work, nevertheless retain their hidden agenda of 'saving souls' rather than 'stimulating self-help and community development'.

Other commentators indicated that churches in working-class districts often have their congregations 'bussed in' from outside the area and that the clergy are 'incomers who do not live locally.' There was considerable consensus that 'many churches do not reflect the local community in which they are based.' One particular speaker at one of the seminars was the Loyalist paramilitary leader Gusty Spence who spoke with considerable conviction about the 'lack of present-day response to the social needs of the community' by the churches. Referring to the notorious denominational diversity of Ulster Protestant culture he lamented the 'fragmentation of the Protestant church', which he felt had 'a negative impact on its people'. He indicated his belief that 'a few ministers with a community conscience have been left by their superiors to plough a lonely furrow without understanding let alone help.'

The negative views expressed in these paragraphs may fail to take account of the deep spiritual and practical help being given to members and associates by traditional faith-based groups in working-class communities. Nonetheless, it is important for the church to recognise its poor standing among a number of committed individuals in the voluntary and community sector who would be better kept as allies rather than critics.

Church and the Community: The Coleraine Area

Derek Bacon's investigation of church-going and voluntary activity in the predominantly Protestant area in and around Coleraine in the summer of 1996 produced interesting conclusions. Eighty-seven of the 90 churches in the region agreed to take part in the survey and although it was undertaken in a part of Northern Ireland with a considerable mix of urban, rural and coastal populations and a much greater concentration of wealth than the Lower Ravenhill area of inner-city Belfast, nonetheless the results make for useful reading.

Bacon found that in the 87 churches in question, 7,359 hours of voluntary work were clocked up in an average week. Altogether, 1,025 people were engaged in pastoral care and visitation of church members

and 1,261 volunteers took care of church-based children's groups and youth organisations on a weekly basis, looking after 7,800 young people. When it came to involvement in the Coleraine community, a number of church members were also involved in such activities as visiting the elderly of the neighbourhood, operating parent and toddler groups and working with unchurched teenagers. Some others were involved in local charities outside the immediate church context.

However, the interviewer found a significant trend. When it came down to measuring their own or their church's contribution to the 'social well-being' of the wider community, as opposed to their church community, most respondents had great difficulty in replying. Only 15% of interviewees were able to make any such quantitative estimate. The concept of the church member making a contribution to civic well-being as opposed to the life and witness of his or her church was a foreign one. As Bacon indicated, 'the obvious individual warmth, generosity, friendliness and mutual concern within many a church is often to be contrasted with an apparent weakness of a sense of corporate responsibility for those outside, or of any obligation to build with other groups in the local community towards common goals.' For example, the churches' often substantial real estate was largely used only for the congregations' own purposes. Over 70% of Coleraine's church premises were never – or only rarely – made available for use by other bodies in the community. Less than 5% of churches made their premises available to others on a regular basis.

Bacon felt a conceptual gap was also to be seen in Coleraine Council's recent social and economic audit, which acknowledged absolutely no work done by local churches in its account of voluntary work within the community.

Bacon's conclusion was that individual churches had a habit of 'doing their own thing' and acting mainly as sanctuaries for their own particular company of believers. Only 2% of respondents felt their church had 'a great deal' of contact with other churches in the area. Forty-one percent reckoned there was either 'not much' or 'no contact' at all. Alongside this, churches made little contact with other obvious potential partners in the pursuit of civic well-being. Only 2% of respondents believed their church to be making a 'great deal' of contact with local voluntary and community groups, whilst 72% reckoned that their church had 'no contact' or 'not much' at all. None of the respondents felt that there was a 'great deal' of contact between their church and such statutory bodies such as the Probation Service, Housing Executive and child welfare agencies. Eighty-five percent believed their church to have 'no contact' whatsoever.

This set of figures should not invalidate the fine 'voluntary work' that many Coleraine church members were in fact doing, albeit unwittingly. Nor should they eclipse the more innovative and collaborative work now being done by a number of local churches in Coleraine but they do seem to reveal a recent legacy of minimal interaction between many individual churches and poor avenues of contact with other players in the voluntary promotion of local civic well-being. These research findings may be placed alongside statistics which reveal considerable involvement of Coleraine's Christians in voluntary missionary activity overseas. Fifty-one percent of churches had members who had left Northern Ireland in order to offer themselves for a life of dedicated – and often very practical – voluntary work in such far-flung places as South America, the Caribbean, Africa, India, Thailand, China, the Philippines and the former Soviet republics.[15]

Disillusionment with the Church? Newtownards and Elsewhere

Tony Macaulay's survey of church and community in the predominantly Protestant town of Newtownards was conducted in 2003 and complements the work done by Bacon and Acheson and the findings of the seminars on community work in Protestant areas. His report examined the work of 28 churches in the town and found remarkably little sustained interaction between these individual congregations. Indeed, a significant number of local clergy had never even met one another. Most churches also had either no contact or very little contact with local community and voluntary groups, with the notable exception of the town's Link Family and Community Centre, which had originally been set up by Regent Street Presbyterian Church but by that time had a much wider Christian base.

Most secular community, voluntary and statutory groups were dissatisfied with the current low level of church involvement with them on common projects. One interviewee commented, 'We tried unsuccessfully to get clergy onto the inter-agency forum on domestic violence. There is a high level of domestic violence in this area…so the churches should be taking it seriously.' One other person expressed the view that the churches 'only get involved in community work to access funds for their buildings' and offered the verdict that they 'only get involved with vulnerable people to convert them.' Another community worker felt that Christians had 'little or no impact or interest in disadvantaged housing estates' and the incisive view by one interviewee that some churches do 'evangelistic commando raids' on deprived estates while others, who happened to be located in these areas, 'tend to be made up of a majority of members who no longer live in the estate.'

However, in order to balance these negative verdicts, it must be said that some Christians in this town are now actually at the forefront of contemporary Christian community work in Northern Ireland, both through the work of churches rooted in Loyalist estates and through the aforementioned Link project.

In their own defence, some church leaders explained to Macaulay that they were suspicious of becoming involved with community groups in some of Newtownards' more difficult housing estates because of a fear of their paramilitary leadership. Some churches indicated that they had had their fingers burnt in the past when engaging with such organisations. Loyalist paramilitary influence in a number of estates has hitherto presented an intimidating prospect. As a Newtownards community audit, conducted for the Link Centre in 2005, pointed out, 'Paramilitary organisations are often perceived as policing the estates rather then the Police Service of Northern Ireland.'[16]

The thoughts of community workers in other parts of the province, who operate outside a faith-based context, are also revealing. One senior youth worker employed by a local council in County Antrim offered her views in a recent interview. If her analysis is wholly accurate then it pinpoints deeply serious limitations to the church's capacity for contemporary social engagement in that area. Even if the picture it presents is not entirely accurate, it still reveals a remarkably negative perception of the Christian community by a respected local professional, which must be taken seriously by church leaders:

> Churches are a crucial part of the Protestant community and so they should be addressing the issues that working-class Protestants are facing but they are not. They've got to get 'down and dirty' with the people. In my experience, the churches are reluctant to meet with paramilitaries. They pay lip service to getting involved with loyalists but in actuality very few of them are really ready to work with bodies like the Ulster Political Research Group who seem to be trying to steer loyalists towards peace and prosperity.
>
> The churches have always been interested in the 'nice' kids and consequently the 'bad' youngsters

have always been thrown out of the church youth clubs. This only antagonises these 'difficult' ones and it certainly means that – both as teenagers and in later life – they will not see the church as a place they can go or be welcome. If you ask me the churches live in a great big white ivory tower.

They also offer little to entice problem young people and problem adults in through their doors. I mean you have to have something better than indoor bowls! The churches also have to learn to work with people, not for them. They mustn't come across as a bunch of middle-class do-gooders. Perhaps they feel they will lose control if they open their doors more widely. They have to come to local communities and say 'What do we need to do for you?' and they need to pick the right people in their congregations to do the outreach. They mustn't use people who feel that doing this work will get them a step or two closer to heaven. These workers will need to be strong and open minded and, above all, trained. They could start by sending out their youth workers with our North Eastern Education and Library Board youth workers to see the kind of lives many young people live on the estates.

There has to be respect built up on both sides if the church and the community are to work together. One thing the churches could have done a lot more was to offer their buildings as nego-tiating spaces during the loyalist feuds that have been happening. They need to see that the halls and other real estate that they have could be of service to the whole community and not just be used for the church members themselves.

There is, I am afraid, too much indifference to working with council officers like ourselves to tackle social problems. For instance, I recently tried to get as many as possible of the local clergymen to come to an event where we could discuss the problem of racism, which has emerged in working-class estates in the borough. I organised it as a working lunch and I had some plans to put to the churches. For instance I wanted to facilitate contacts between migrants and local congregations. I would be prepared to help make the introductions. I thought maybe the churches could co-operate on producing a pack to give to migrants to indicate what they could offer. Out of the 60 churches in the area, only eight ministers came along. Most of those who were absent did not even email me to offer apologies for their absence.

What I would say to the local churches is this: 'You have a ready-made audience and huge facilities. You could be spreading the word and giving a hand on so many different key issues but I get the impression you would be happier giving a five-pound note than five minutes of your time. Open your doors. Get to know the faces of the local people who don't go near your church. Build rapport. Reach out! [17]

Another anonymous interviewee – this time a Presbyterian minister – offered his thoughts on what he believed was the failure of the church to stay close to the people:

In the past, Christians wanted to distance themselves from the violence of the paramilitaries. Perhaps, though, we should have stayed closer to the people in Loyalist areas. Roman Catholic clergy seem to have managed to do that kind of thing rather more successfully. Maybe it's due to the way in which the Reformed Church focuses on its own 'gathered community' rather than the total community out there in which it is situated. Very often the minister's extent of involvement in that local community consists of little more than being on the board of governors of the local school. Mean-while the church halls sit empty during the day and are used only by church-based groups. Where we do serve the community, we tend to do it too much on our own terms. Possibly we need a new "theology of community" in order to help us to engage. [18]

Does Partnership with Secular Groups Mean Compromise?

Recent failures by the church in Northern Ireland may not be attributable to a unique failure of either vision or adaptability. Northern Ireland has gone through a long period of civil conflict, which has stultified all kinds of creativity and risk-taking throughout society. The notable absence of a concept of a shared civic society, to which churches should contribute, might be expected in a place that has been, since the onset of violence in 1969, a deeply divided and fearful polity. The evolution of devolved government in Northern Ireland may help to create a common, civic identity which could enable some Protestant church-goers to possess a stronger sense of a 'society' to which they owe more than just an evangelistic duty, beyond the walls of their chosen church. If so, these church members and their leaders may feel able to grasp hold of current working-class needs in a way that does fresh justice to the ethos which pervaded earlier phases of the Irish Protestant and Evangelical traditions.

However, the sense of wariness when faced with new community challenges should not be under-

estimated. Even those Christian leaders who favour an integration of the social and the personal gospels have articulated their deep concerns. For the Presbyterian minister Norman Hamilton, operating on the troubled streets of North Belfast, the secular community development movement in his district is a strong force to be carefully scrutinised before being considered as a potential partner. Over 300 independently constituted community groups appeared on the mailing list of the North Belfast Partnership Board in 2001 and Hamilton's fear has been that 'partnership arrangements with local community groups could well be seen as endorsement of the secular agenda of these groups and as drawing away very limited and declining church resources from the primary task of evangelism and Christian discipleship' yet, as he points out 'failure to relate positively and properly to these same community groups will further reinforce the perception that neither the local church nor the gospel itself has any relevance to ordinary people who have suffered a great deal in the civil conflict.'

Hamilton notes that the 'biblical injunctions to care for people in need' have to be reworked to cope with the 'new parameters of community development and partnership expectations' but that crucial biblical morals must not be abandoned in the process. For instance, the communitarian principle of 'inclusiveness' must not be absorbed by the church to the extent that it promotes the viewpoint that all ideas and values held by citizens are of equal worth. Christian teaching clearly proclaims a range of right and wrong behaviours.

For instance, Christians who are involved with secular partners in the area of youth work will find it difficult to accept the practice of freely available teenage contraception – a liberal sexual guideline to which most conservative Christians would have deep moral objections – even though a compassionate response to underage pregnancy would, nonetheless, be entirely consonant with the gospel.

Evangelicals might also argue that the doctrine of community 'empowerment' is problematic for Christian theology, if its fundamental assumption is that tackling society's structural injustices and promoting peoples' sense of self-worth will be enough to sort out human problems. The Evangelical analysis of the human dilemma focuses much more closely on the issue of an individual's alienation from God, which can only properly be dealt with through personal acceptance of Christ as Saviour and Lord.

Hamilton sees real dangers for churchgoers who get sucked into the time-consuming and energy-sapping world of community involvement. This concerns the 'over-stretching' of church members who 'are so fully engaged in the daily routine of church life and have very little spare capacity.' What is being pointed out here is surely of considerable validity. Evangelical churches, in particular, expect high levels of commitment. Involvement in mid-week meetings as well as weekend activities is often considered normative. The strain thereby placed on family life, in a world where jobs and schooling already eat up many hours of both the parents' and the children's time, can be considerable. The notion of additional Christian tasks and responsibilities, connected to a fresh phase of church outreach is too much for many church members to contemplate. [19]

Community Work and the Evangelical Ethos

Is community involvement mainly seen by Evangelicals as a means to reach new converts with 'the gospel'? That seems to be the rationale behind outreach activities for a number of local churches that have embraced greater community involvement. One particular Belfast Evangelical congregation, surveyed in 2001, saw the chief benefit of its local 'social action' as being its potential for exposing 'more people to the preaching of the gospel', citing the example of its neighbourhood Parent and Toddler group. Many parents who have brought their children to this group have then sent them to the church's Sunday school and subsequently 'some of these parents have been attracted to our services, enjoyed the experience of worship and have come to personal faith in Christ.'

As this minister also pointed out, his church eldership firmly believe that 'they dare not separate evangelism from social action', giving as his example a project undertaken in a local Loyalist housing estate which was inspired by the motto 'We need to be in the community to win them for Christ'. Within the premises which the church has been acquiring for its outreach work the aim is to provide education in computer skills, an after-school homework club and other beneficial facilities. However, most importantly of all, the premises is to be a centre for 'preaching of the gospel and Bible studies…Our journey into social action has not weakened our evangelistic ethos, rather [it] has strengthened and broadened our approach, and the number of opportunities to share the gospel.'[20]

The drive to evangelise through community work is an understandable and obvious outcome of the Evangelical perception that humankind is in grave danger of being eternally separated from God. But is there likely to be a problem with what one commentator referred to earlier in this chapter as a 'hidden agenda' behind social engagement, namely 'saving souls' without due attention to the more prosaic but vital tasks of 'stimulating self-help and community development'? Is an intensely evangelistic subtext not likely to awaken suspicion among many of the people in a disadvantaged neighbourhood that their community is being helped for what they might regard as ulterior motives? Would sticking to an 'old-fashioned' preaching of the gospel not be less inauthentic than this?

Could it be that community work, with all its challenges, ought to be undertaken for its own sake, because it is, biblically, the right thing to do in a hurting world? Is it possible that active care for those in social, cultural and economic need is to be undertaken because it is in itself an act of righteousness and compassion, not dissimilar to the medical care offered by a Christian nurse or doctor or the education offered by a Christian teacher, which needs no secondary justification in terms of evangelism or a church-building mission, even though these latter tasks are also very deeply important?

In other words, is it feasible for Ulster's Evangelicals to retain a Christian emphasis on the urgent message of personal rebirth through reconciliation to God in Christ, alongside a mission to the wider community that is rooted in the simple desire to make this society a better place? And if so, is there a prophetic role for the church to play in challenging the structures and processes in that society which perpetuate deep inequality, injustice and exclusion?

Growth in Funding Opportunities

There are opportunities as never before for financial help with social action projects by faith-based groups. The environment for voluntary action has been altered in the United Kingdom within recent times. The state has increasingly withdrawn from frontline delivery of services to needy communities. Instead there has been a public policy of 'mainstreaming' the voluntary sector by the government and a willingness to provide a measure of funding to back up this process. Churches are now seen by government as some of the most ideally placed agencies for delivering care and support to those who are in difficulty, at the local level.

The role played by churches in this scheme of things is more complex in a religiously conflicted region such as Northern Ireland. During the Troubles, the central government saw Northern Ireland's churches as the ancient custodians of ethnic loyalty and presumed that their current task within Ulster society was to redress that dim legacy by positive 'reconciliation' initiatives across the 'sectarian divide'. However, as government-sponsored initiatives such as the Renewing Communities project clearly show, churches are now being recognised for what they offer by way of social capital to the local communities in which they are based or to which they may have some access. Churches still provide a sense of inclusion, identity and shared values to many of their members and claim to have a message of deep spiritual hope and collective support for the troubled and the disadvantaged. Church groups are now recognised by the government as possessing a lot of 'human capital' in terms of talent, expertise and volunteer energy and insomuch as they also possess significant physical infrastructure that can benefit a local community, such as church halls and sports facilities.' [21]

To draw down these funds, Northern Ireland's churches must take on an innovative, positive and stable role as providers of 'social capital' within Protestant working-class communities. They must be prepared to work alongside other partners in the voluntary and statutory sector. They probably have to be prepared to 'get down and dirty', as one interviewee has phrased it, sometimes operating with people who are not easy to handle and less easy to love. Those believers who get involved will need to feel reconnected with the great tradition of Christian community engagement, working within new parameters yet holding onto distinctly biblical values.

This chapter has asked some questions about the church's capacity for a new wave of radical engagement. One aspect that will require careful consideration is that in the Protestant communities where need is greatest, an allegiance to Loyalism is invariably present. The next chapter attempts to look at this issue.

[1] Information on Belfast City Mission courtesy of Bobby Foster, Spectrum Centre, Shankill, 2007.

[2] Statistics on the history of the Shankill area, courtesy of Bobby Foster, Spectrum Centre, Shankill, 2007.

[3] Information on Campbell Street Mission, courtesy of Bobby Foster, Spectrum Centre, Shankill, 2007.

[4] Dudley Levistone Cooney, *The Methodists in Ireland: A Short History*, (Columba Press, 2001) pp 180-229.

[5] Finlay Holmes, *Our Irish Presbyterian Heritage*, (Publications Committee of the Presbyterian Church in Ireland, 1985) pp 115-118.

[6] Information on current church-going and religious allegiance may be found throughout Chapter 2 of Claire Mitchell's *Religion and Politics in Northern Ireland: Boundaries of Belonging and Belief*, (Ashgate Press, 2005).

[7] Tony Macaulay's survey was conducted in 2003 for the 'Youthnet' organisation. The information used here was obtained courtesy of the author.

[8] This information may be found in Chapter 2 of Clare Mitchell's *Religion, Identity and Politics in Northern Ireland: Boundaries of Belonging and Belief*, (Ashgate Press, 2005).

[9] See Ian McAllister's article 'Driven to Disaffection: Religious Independents in Northern Ireland' Ark Update, Issue 41 (November 2005) at http://www.ark.ac.uk/publications/updates/. Accessed 20 November 2007.

[10] This survey was reported in *The Irish News*, 10 December, 2007.

[11] Norman Hamilton, 'The Bible, Church and Community' in *Engaging with the Community*, (Presbyterian Church in Ireland, 2001).

[12] Derek Bacon, *Revitalising Civil Society in Northern Ireland*, (University of Ulster, Centre for Voluntary Action Studies, 2001) p 5.

[13] A written summation of Christine Acheson's work was loaned to me by Connor Mulholland, Belfast.

[14] A selection of the comments generated during these seminars was loaned to me by Connor Mulholland, Belfast.

[15] The findings of the survey of church activity in the Coleraine area are to be found throughout Derek Bacon's '*Splendid and Disappointing': Churches, Voluntary Action and Social Capital in Northern Ireland*, (University of Ulster, Centre for Voluntary Action Studies, 1998).

[16] Tony Macaulay's Report on Inter-Church and Church-Community Relations in Newtownards in 2003 and his Newtownards Community Relations Audit of 2004/5 were loaned to me by the author.

[17] Interview conducted in Newtownabbey, September 2007.

[18] Interview conducted in Belfast, October 2008.

[19] Norman Hamilton, 'The Bible, the Church and the Community' in *Engaging with the Community*, (Presbyterian Church in Ireland, 2001) pp 11-18.

[20] Ken McBride, 'Our Church, Our Community: a Personal Perspective' in *Engaging with the Community*, (Presbyterian Church in Ireland, 2001) pp 19-22.

[21] A summary of the renewed government interest in church within the community was found in Derek Bacon's, '*Revitalising Civil Society in Northern Ireland: Social capital formation in three faith-based organisations*' at www.ncvo-vol.org.uk. Accessed 25 November 2007.

3

a history of conflict

This part of the study will seek to define Loyalism and highlight some of its different strands. It will note the close relationship of some Protestant churches with Loyalist culture. It will also try to clarify why the thought of a new and incisive engagement with Loyalists may cause some churches a degree of trepidation.

There can be no doubt that Loyalist culture brings out widely different responses in church circles. Many sincere Christian believers are happy to fly a Union Jack in their garden and march with an Orange Lodge, believing that Loyalism pays tribute to a Great Britain that was a historic defender of the Reformed Protestant faith. Others – particularly from a more tranquil middle-class background – feel a deep wariness about getting too close both to Loyalism and to its adherents. This may be due to scepticism about Loyalist ideology. It may also be due to the way the Troubles were fought out at a territorial level in Loyalist working-class communities – in a manner not experienced within most middle-class circles. In many Loyalist communities antagonisms were and are intense. Lacking the expressive nuances and conceptual guile of the professional classes, working-class Protestants can articulate those antagonisms in a very stark way that can frighten the middle-class outsider, Christian or otherwise.

Defining Loyalism

Defining what 'Loyalism' actually means is a contentious matter. Numerous political commentators have used the term simply to denote a working class form of the Unionism which aspires to keep Northern Ireland British. However, for one or two astute, if anonymous, observers of Protestant culture who were interviewed in the course of this project, Loyalism is a term carefully used by the middle classes simply to separate themselves from expressions of Unionism among the working classes which they neither like nor understand. One other unnamed interviewee suggested that the term originated with Gusty Spence, the father figure of the modern-day paramilitary Ulster Volunteer Force, and that it was a word which he idealistically wished to see supplanting 'Protestant' in paramilitary circles, in an attempt to avoid the accusation of old-fashioned sectarianism.

The academic Steve Bruce suggests that, 'Loyalists are Ulster Protestant first and British second' as opposed to what he calls the 'Ulster British' who are 'British first and only secondarily root their identity in Ulster'. He also argues that 'for many Protestants in Northern Ireland, Ulster Loyalism has displaced the Ulster Britishness which was common prior to the present conflict.'[1] For local analysts Peter Shirlow and Mark McGovern, the term Loyalist is 'usually engaged to refer to the more intemperate and/or populist supporters of the Unionist cause; those who are willing to countenance draconian state action or the use of paramilitary violence to sustain the Northern Ireland state.'[2]

For the purposes of this publication, Loyalism within the Protestant working class will be studied in two main forms. Firstly, in the shape of an ostensibly religious affirmation, connected to the Loyal Orders – the Orange institution, the Royal Black Preceptory and the Apprentice Boys of Derry – which guard a proud if contested version of the Protestant heritage and a memory of Ulster's heyday during the most glorious days of the British Empire. Connected to this is a vibrant but often intimidating 'band' culture, which supplies the martial music for parades. The issue of these parades and their 're-routing' away from Nationalist areas during the summer marching season has continued to be a thorn in the side of the peace process, bringing conflict and chaos to Loyalist areas on several occasions.

Secondly, there is affiliation to and support for the Loyalist paramilitary organisations. The two most significant of these have been the Ulster Defence Association and the Ulster Volunteer Force. A sizeable number of those who died in the Troubles met their end at the hands of members of these two organisations.

However, even in an era of ceasefires, demilitarisation, decommissioning and devolved government, the Loyalist paramilitaries have continued to play a role in the life of many Protestant working-class people, often offering a sense of belonging, sometimes providing a surprisingly progressive political vision but also acting as an illegal police force and too often delivering a form of drug-trade gangsterism.

Most calling themselves Loyalists are, for most of the time, peaceful citizens, whom it would be wrong to single out for demonisation. Nonetheless, the history of Loyalism is a key part of the local story of civil conflict and it would be naïve not to admit that it has often been shaped and characterised by civil disruption and the threat of violence – hence the fears not just of many Ulster Catholics but also of those Protestants who have been born, educated, domiciled and 'churched' in altogether gentler or less politically committed circumstances.

The Challenge of Relating to the Loyal Orders

Estimates of numbers in the Orange Order vary greatly, with one commentator suggesting that in 2001 there were 40,000 members,[3] whereas another source indicates a membership in that year of 75,000.[4] Added to these figures are the large numbers of men and women involved in marching bands which form such a key feature of the hundreds of parades which take place all across Northern Ireland every summer or those who throng the route to watch a parade go by.[5]

The Order traces its roots to the 1790s and the famous 'Battle of the Diamond' near Loughgall in County Armagh, when a number of the local Protestants clashed with local Catholics and, shortly afterwards, an organisation was created to protect Irish Protestant faith, rights and culture. The name of William of Orange was invoked – the Dutchman invited to take the British throne in the late 17th century and whose victory over the Catholic James II at the Battle of the Boyne in 1690, secured the Protestant ascendancy in Ireland for over two centuries.

The Order is keen to point out to all enquirers that, in the words of the historian, ATQ Stewart, 'its birth was not the cause but the consequence of prolonged and severe sectarian conflict'[6] and that its political desires could well be summed up as 'civil and religious liberty for all: special privileges for none.' The Orange commentator, Brian Kennaway, points to this strongly religious purpose and ethos of the Order, which he sees as having been compromised in recent years. However, there can be no question that the Orange institution is also adamantly pro-British in its politics. Joining a local lodge can thus make a strongly Unionist political statement though it may also constitute a desire to be a part of a social club or to continue a much-cherished family heritage.

The most visible features of the Order on parade are its banners and collarettes, each covered in Orangeism's special insignia and iconic emblems. Its most audible features are the four types of band – pipe, flute, brass and accordion – and the famous Lambeg drum with its goatskin drumhead and distinctive percussive rhythms. The Order proudly points out that its parading culture, which is so often berated for inflaming sectarian tensions, serves three main functions: it bears public witness to the Reformed Christian faith, it enacts a solemn remembrance of dead members – especially those killed in the Troubles – and it acts as a celebration of Irish Protestant culture.[7]

Many Protestant clergy are happy to be chaplains to Orange Lodges. Many others are striving for a 'neutral' political stance in a divided province, and are now wary of the Order. However, the reality is that key members of his or her congregation may be in an Orange Lodge and there is the possibility that at least one traditional Orange Service is held in the church each year. Negotiating the issues to do with this show of 'Loyalty' may prove to be difficult for clerics who wish to avoid political identification of the faith with local politics but also desire to cause no offence to esteemed church members.

Particularly problematic for many Protestant church leaders, has been the Loyalist attempt to defend Orange culture against perceived challenges from Nationalism during the 1990s and the early years of the 21st century. This has led to scenes of fighting and social chaos on the streets of Northern Ireland as the government has striven to mediate between Orangemen and Nationalist opponents concerning those contentious parades which pass close to Catholic areas, of which by far the most important has been the one from Drumcree to Portadown each July. Protestant working-class areas of the province were the ones most affected by rioting and civil disorder during the Drumcree conflagrations and during the reactions to other re-routing decisions made by the government-appointed Parades Commission. The most notable one of these involved altering a route through the Whiterock area of Belfast in September 2005, which led to widespread violence, including an assault by Loyalist gunmen on the police. Commercial premises were burnt out, vehicles hijacked and ordinary citizens attacked while going about their daily lives. It seemed to many onlookers that Loyalists were in fact destroying their own areas out of political frustration and cultural despair at a 'peace process' that seemed to them to be all gain for Nationalists and all loss for

Unionists. For many middle-class Christians who watched much of this violence on television or who had their car hijacked by an angry mob, the fury of thwarted Orange culture was and is hard to understand.

New or renewed connections made by middle-class and 'middle-of-the-road' churches with neighbouring Protestant working-class communities will have to be based around an understanding of the upheaval brought about by these episodes of Loyalist violence and must grasp the deep opposition to the Parades Commission, which since 1997 has been able to decide which parades can march where in Northern Ireland. Opposition is based on the sense that the commission is a 'quango' and that its decisions can overturn years of Orange tradition on the whim of local Nationalist leaders.

Leaders of community engagement initiatives in Loyalist areas should also bear in mind the serious rifts within the Order over the levels of violence incurred during Drumcree, Whiterock and other disturbances. Some Orangemen in a local community may have been very 'pro' the Drumcree protest or they may have been against it, at least during its most violent phase. Among the most vehement critics of the Order's leadership in recent times has been Brian Kennaway, himself a member of the Order, who has lamented what he sees as the paranoia and anger of much contemporary Orangeism:

> Everyone is said, and seen, to be against us. The government is often portrayed as having no interest in Northern Ireland and as "wanting rid of us". The Northern Ireland Office is perceived as the agent of the government and is therefore demonised as "the enemy"…the greatest venom is reserved for the media, described as "no friend of ours". [8]

Recently, attempts have been made by the Order to improve its relationship with the media and to boost its own self-confidence through educational and cultural activities and an alliance with the increasingly visible 'Ulster Scots' network. It has also sought to take a leadership role in advocating the rights of deprived Protestant communities and in arguing for the allocation of resources to help build 'community development capacity' in these areas.

A key dilemma for churches wishing to reach out genuinely to Loyalist communities is how exactly to interact, not just with local Orange lodges, but with the local marching bands, which gain such devotion from their members yet often present an aggressive demeanour and can bring a crowd of drunken followers in their wake. If speculative friendships develop, there may well be a request to open up the church's sanctuary for the first time to an Orange service or indeed to let a band practise in a church hall, on promise of good behaviour. There are obvious reasons why a church that has hitherto had no truck with Orangeism might think this a cultural compromise of the purity of the gospel within a divided society. Yet the rejection of such links may, quite arguably, help put many working-class Loyalists beyond the reach of the local church.

Orangeism feels on the defensive on several fronts. It no longer draws on many middle-class and professional Protestants who used to provide leadership. Orange Halls have also often come under sectarian attack as visible and vulnerable emblems of Unionism. For these reasons, the Order often represents a troubled and not always articulate working-class Loyalist culture that believes the Protestant church should take a much more positive response to 'its own people' and not 'betray its own heritage'. Such proclamations of betrayal can be frightening to Christians who are seeking to walk what they see as a 'middle road' – particularly so in a society where the traitor is such a figure of hate and the middle of the road can be seen as a place of evil compromise.[9]

However, as already indicated, different kinds of Orangeman exist. There is the strident Portadown Orangeman of Drumcree Hill and the urban Orangeman from working-class Belfast who is now being encouraged with his family to see the Twelfth of July march through the city as an exuberant 'Orangefest'. Then there is the Orangeman to be found in so many rural communities, who lives side by side with his Catholic neighbour and where a close Orange link with the local church helps define the local lodge as a religious rather than an overtly political body.

One spokesman for a deeply rural branch of the Order may be left to make his case for an Orangeism that seeks good community relationships, rejects violence and sees absolutely no conflict between lodge membership and the Christian faith:

> Here where I am based, in the Clogher valley, there is a close relationship between the church and the Orange Order. Sometimes a minister comes out from the city to a rural parish and thinks he can change all that. We can usually explain the situation and he comes around to our way of thinking. You see, in rural areas like ours, Orangeism is purely a Christian organisation. On the Twelfth of July, the Tyrone Orange Lodge endeavours to ensure that there are no political speeches made at the demonstration.
>
> Sadly, in recent times the organisation has lost a number of what you might call more middle

class people. Drumcree has been responsible for that. We are trying our best to reverse that trend and hold on to our young professionals. We would have no connection to paramilitaries whatsoever. When we saw paramilitary representation at a Belfast parade recently, we sent a letter to the Grand Lodge saying how much we deplored that situation.

Tyrone Orange Vision was founded in 2000 and has tried to rekindle the memory of the days when Orange and Green could exist in harmony in the countryside. Sadly the Troubles changed all that. A lot of small halls were attacked and a lot had to close up. We now want to display to Protestant and Roman Catholic alike a positive vision of the Orange Order. We run workshops in neutral venues, exploring the Orange heritage, which are open for all to attend. We want to open up a lot of the halls again and make them venues where young people can enjoy some healthy recreational activities.[10]

The Ulster Volunteer Force

Various brands of paramilitarism which flourished during the Troubles have passed from the scene including the Orange Volunteers and the Vanguard Service Corps. Two large bodies have continued to be important – the Ulster Defence Association (UDA) and the Ulster Volunteer Force (UVF), the latter group being closely allied to the much smaller Red Hand Commando. The UVF and the UDA are solidly, if not exclusively, working class in membership.

The paramilitary group which claims the oldest pedigree is the Ulster Volunteer Force, founded as a modern organisation in the 1960s but boasting continuity with the body of that name which was created to fight the plans for a Dublin parliament in the years leading up to the Great War, even though the original UVF was a much larger organisation and included Protestants from all sections of society. In due course thousands of the old UVF men joined the British Army and were annihilated at the Somme, giving the modern-day UVF a deep empathy with the sufferings and heroism of that particular battle and a proud sense of themselves as an armed unit, following strict codes of discipline – even though this self-perception may sit at odds with the chaotic sprees of killing which were sometimes the UVF's trademark.

The present-day UVF began its campaign of violence with the killing of two Catholics – John Patrick Scullion and Peter Ward – under the leadership of an ex-soldier, Gusty Spence, in 1966, stimulated by a desire to quell Nationalist self-confidence in a year that saw the 50th anniversary of the Easter Rising. A campaign of bombings and shootings on both sides of the border followed in the late 1960s and early 1970s as the UVF attempted to destabilise moderate Unionism in Northern Ireland and to counter the revolutionary new self-assertiveness of Irish Catholics, at first manifested in the shape of the Civil Rights movement and then latterly in the militant shape of the Provisional Irish Republican Army (IRA). By mid-1972, as Northern Ireland descended into the hell of widespread civil conflict, the UVF was 2,000 strong and committed to a campaign of killing which targeted ordinary Catholics. This was done, according to the UVF's leaders, partly because IRA volunteers were very hard to target and partly in the belief that the only way in which the IRA could be forced to give up their 'armed struggle' on behalf of the Catholic community would be by making that community recognise the cost of shelter given to the perpetrators of Republican violence.

In 1974, the UVF was also responsible for the single most violent day thus far of the Troubles, when it exploded car bombs in Dublin and Monaghan, killing 33 civilians. During the rest of the 1970s, numerous other killings took place, including the infamous assault on the Miami Showband, but by the end of the decade a serious government attempt to crush the organisation resulted in a quarter of the members being placed behind bars. The 1980s saw the emergence within the ranks of the UVF of the 'Shankill Butchers' whose sectarian killings were conducted with grim ferocity in West and North Belfast; however, by the end of the decade the Ulster Volunteer Force was beginning to target, with greater regularity and effect, a number of Sinn Fein and IRA activists. By the early 1990s, the organisation was in fact 'out-killing' the Provisional IRA and it is widely held in UVF circles that it was this highly accurate paramilitary campaign that was influential in persuading the Republicans to abandon their 'armed struggle' and proclaim a ceasefire in 1994.

In October of that year, in response to the Provisionals' ceasefire, announced a few weeks previously, the UVF and their fellow Loyalist paramilitaries called a halt to their campaign, in a carefully worded statement delivered by Gusty Spence, who had been such a seminal and presiding figure for the group since the campaign in the 1960s. In this statement, Spence offered 'abject and true remorse' for the hurt caused by Loyalist violence throughout the previous three decades. Spence's influence continued to be felt in the post-ceasefire years as several of his protégés in the prison camp at Long Kesh took up positions of leadership in the Progressive Unionist Party – a UVF-linked political grouping that attempted to offer a much more left-wing version of the customary pro-union political analysis of Ulster politics. This political slant was very much in keeping with what had surfaced from time to time throughout the long years of militarism

In Memory
Of
All of Ulster's Fallen
1914 – 1918
1939 – 1945
The recent conflict

...cers and Volunteers
...NDO

– a genuine interest in critiquing both the Unionism of established privilege and the Paisley-led Unionism of Fundamentalist Protestantism.[11]

The years since the ceasefires have often been deeply disturbing ones for the UVF. One of the organisation's most ruthless leaders, Billy Wright, led a breakaway group known as the Loyalist Volunteer Force (LVF) and rivalry between the LVF and UVF occurred on several occasions. Even more vicious was the feud between the UVF and the UDA. This conflict had surfaced regularly throughout the Troubles but in the early years of the 21st century it would result in several lost lives and in terrible social divisions within such communities as Loyalist West Belfast, with the lower Shankill area becoming a UDA redoubt and the upper Shankill featuring as a UVF stronghold. Christian community work in such areas may still expect an encounter with the bitter fall-out of this feud.

However, having experimented in its East Antrim area with a Conflict Transformation project inspired in large measure by the work of UVF veteran Billy Mitchell, the UVF decided in 2007 to 'roll out' this model across Ulster, whereby former volunteers would cease to engage in all paramilitary activities and either seek 'normal' employment opportunities or involve themselves in local community work. Consequently in May 2007, the UVF announced that all recruitment, training and targeting had ceased and its active service units were to be 'deactivated' although its guns would not be handed over for decommissioning but rather placed 'beyond reach'. The UVF as an army seemed, at last, to have gone away, but not the pride which many UVF men and their families felt that their organisation had fought successfully against a Nationalist enemy and then made a resourceful transformation into a distinctive brand of politics.[12]

There is a challenge here for many church members who had the good fortune to avoid the worst of the Troubles and whose only loyalty to a local militia was to the security forces. In some UVF-dominated estates, most of the male population has at some stage been involved with the organisation. Murals depicting UVF men as heroes have, until recently, looked down from every gable end. A UVF club may be at the centre of social life. In connecting with the inhabitants of such an estate, how do church members handle paramilitary allegiance in a way that shows empathy and understanding yet does not appear to condone the paramilitary killings that led to much suffering in the Catholic community?

The Ulster Defence Association

The Ulster Defence Association, which grew out of the various Protestant vigilante groups of the early 1970s, reached a peak in terms of numbers by 1974, when it had some 50,000 members – a figure reduced to 20,000 by 2003.[13] This makes it possibly the largest paramilitary force in the recent history of the western world and yet it is an organisation which has been written about and studied a lot less than other major players in the Ulster conflict.

The UDA was created in the late summer of 1971. The contexts in those early days were several. There was the increasingly ferocious IRA bombing and shooting campaign. There was the sense that Britain very possibly wanted to disengage from Northern Ireland while the Irish Republic appeared to be, to a greater or lesser degree, pro-IRA. There was the vulnerability of a Unionist community that had lost its old guardians, the disbanded 'B Special' units of the local constabulary, and there was a general feeling that society was fast heading down the road towards civil war. Its looser and wider bonds of affiliation than those of the UVF – which posed as an elite, secret army – meant that it drew into its ranks a number of men from a trade union and community background. Their influence was felt when the UDA played a key role in the Ulster Workers Council strike of 1974, which so spectacularly brought down the Sunningdale experiment in power sharing with Nationalists.

By this stage the organisation was supplementing its role as a 'defender' of Protestant areas with an offensive campaign of shootings against the Catholic community, beginning in 1971 but carried out after June 1973 by an elite body within the UDA, known as the Ulster Freedom Fighters. From 1972 until the 1980s, the UDA came under the leadership of Andy Tyrie although numerous conflicts between factions and regional 'bosses' sometimes led to feuding and assassination. The organisation was also subject, up until recent times, to allegations of widespread racketeering whilst another key feature was its infiltration by members of the security forces amidst allegations that UDA men carried out killings based on information provided by police and army personnel. The UDA is also open to the allegation of disorganisation and lack of strategy through much of its history. It is arguably the case that in a civil conflict, a pro-state 'terror' group is at a serious disadvantage compared with 'terrorists' who are attacking the status quo, insomuch as many of the best and most capable potential volunteers are likely to be already serving with the well-paid and 'respectable' security forces.

However, at certain key periods, the UDA delivered accurate blows aimed at key Republicans. One such episode, in the early 1980s, disposed of such Republican figures as Miriam Daly and Ronnie Bunting as well as coming close to killing the veteran activist, Bernadette McAliskey. Another such period came after the reorganisation of the UDA in 1989, subsequent to the arrest of many of its 'old guard'. A cellular structure was adopted, consisting of active service units made up of ruthless personnel who had been well-trained and carefully chosen, meaning that the organisation approached the 1994 ceasefires arguably in 'better shape' than ever before. In the words of one UDA commander, 'For the first time we were playing to win'.[14]

Since the ceasefires, the UDA has struggled to come to terms with the peace, having gained a reputation for drug dealing, extortion and crime and having engaged in a deeply damaging feud with the UVF. In recent times of IRA decommissioning and devolved local government, a number of UDA leaders have been seeking ways of disbanding which could be co-ordinated with an injection of British cash into Loyalist areas. Feuds within the UDA about how to go about this process have continued.

What is also intriguing about Loyalist paramilitaries is their episodic involvement in some more innovative spells of Unionist thinking – a feature that if recognised more widely, might help the church to see militant Loyalism as more than just a criminal outfit of thugs. In 1978, the UDA's 'Beyond the Religious Divide' document proposed a Northern Ireland government made up of voluntary coalitions from all the main political parties at a time when many mainstream Unionists opposed such 'compromises'. Then in 1987, a document called Common Sense also dallied with notions of power sharing and called out for a renewal of political vision, suggesting that 'the most dangerous thing to do would be to do nothing.'[15] The key figure behind Common Sense was John McMichael who, until his murder a few months after the publication of the document, was the commander of the UFF but also a proponent of various questionable theories of the racial origins of the 'Ulster Scots' as a people in pre-Celtic Ireland who were known as the 'Cruithin', before their emigration to Scotland and subsequent return to their original 'homeland' as planters. Whereas the UVF had the story of the Somme to hand, in its attempt to create suitable historic inspiration, it is clear that the UDA has struggled to generate a similar project. Apart from the occasional mural of the ancient warrior-hero Cuchullain, Ulster pre-Celtic mythology has not survived in Loyalist street art or folk consciousness while the Somme story continues to flourish.

A sense of the motivation provided for UDA men to go out and kill members of the Nationalist community, is offered by one particular Loyalist, the late Sam Duddy, who on one occasion arrived at a bar he regularly frequented to find that Republicans had subjected it to a gun attack:

> Walking into that bar was like walking into hell, blood, bodies and the screams of the injured. I went over to one of the men who had been shot. He was the son of a friend of mine…sitting with his back propped against the bar, the blood pouring from his head where he's been shot…this other man had been shot in the neck and he was lying beside the phone trying to phone home with the blood pumping out of his neck…all of that strengthened my resolve to get the IRA, and the people who were bringing such wanton destruction to "my country" and "my people". [16]

This type of story could be repeated many times in order to build a sense of what motivated thousands of young working-class Protestants to commit terrible deeds aimed at the Catholic communities that they held responsible for nurturing the IRA gunmen. In making ever deeper contact with Protestant working-class communities, faith-based groups will come face to face with such men as Sam Duddy, with their legacy of 'activism' and, on some occasions, of personal guilt concerning the human consequences of what they did. What must also be faced is the respect in which such men are still held in their communities of origin, for having 'taken the fight to the enemy', often at the risk of incarceration or death. Also, disturbingly, there may appear to be a communal blindness to the hurt done by such men in the course of the Troubles.

Relationships Between the Church and the Paramilitaries

Christian churches will also have to hear the anger that may well be directed at them by Loyalist ex-prisoners who see no sign of the welcoming arms of Christian forgiveness and restorative mercy in this new age of change. Rather there is a sense among many former UDA and UVF men that while 'respectable' Protestants were happy for them to fight their 'dirty war' during the Troubles, they are reluctant to regard them as other than thugs and criminals now, who must be scapegoated for their wrongdoings, even after release from gaol. This seems in contrast to the Catholic community, many of whom have welcomed Republican ex-combatants as peace-makers and made them into key political representatives.[17]

On entering Loyalist working-class areas, church groups unfamiliar with the territory will be in for a number of challenges and surprises. They will witness the perception that the police no longer live in 'our area' and have become a middle-class force, leaving the paramilitaries as an 'on-the-ground' militia who are able, if they so wish, to solve petty crime by the 'traditional' methods of punishment beating or expulsion. There will also be surprise at the disciplined and positive community work that is often undertaken by ex-prisoners and their associates, in ways that defy the stereotype of the Loyalist thug. This may include progressive work on mediation, involving disputes between neighbours and family members. It may also include genuine attempts to find grant aid to repaint belligerent murals and clean up derelict areas or to solve interface disputes before they get out of hand, during the marching season.

It may also be apparent that considerable progress has been made to develop alternatives to violent retribution, in the shape of restorative justice schemes such as the 'Shankill Alternatives' project, which, despite considerable success with local youths, has struggled to gain 'respectability' and official funding. They will also become aware of the painful but necessary attempt by some paramilitaries to 'leave the stage' as a 'community police force' in areas where they too often ruled society with an iron fist. They will also witness the ongoing capacity of the Loyalist parades issue and of tense 'interface' relationships to reignite fuses that, in the interests of all of us, had better remain unlit.

What is in fact fascinating, despite the anti-church sentiments noted above, is the serious if guarded respect for the church among some ex-combatants. It is clear that some Loyalist prisoners encountered a Christian experience while in gaol, even if this was sometimes temporary. Scepticism has been expressed about whether many of these 'conversions' were in fact attempts to gain time off their sentence for 'good behaviour'. However there is a roll call of ex-combatants whose Christian experiences have stood the test of time, including two men who are now clergy within the Presbyterian Church in Ireland and one who has travelled to Japan as a missionary and exercises a function as a chaplain inside a Japanese gaol.[18]

Some UDA Men Interviewed

A number of UDA men were interviewed by the author in Derry in November 2007. For the most part they expressed the opinion that they would go to church for 'a christening, a marriage or a funeral but that would be it.' However, they also expressed the opinion that they would be 'glad to see our children and grandchildren going regularly to church' as it might keep them from choosing the way of life that they had experienced, which in the case of two of the men had involved custodial sentences. The opinion was expressed that they themselves would simply not fit in within a church that they perceived as 'middle class'. One man said that he would be looked down on because of the casual way he dressed.

Yet another man spoke of the 'fantastic' Christians he had met at a local church and noted that 'they gave you respect' rather than 'patronising you'. Most men in this interview session had been 'forced to go to church as children' but then gave it all up as teenagers. Nonetheless, when in gaol, two of the UDA men had gone regularly to religious services, even if it was partly to establish their Protestant identification in a 'mixed' wing.

The discussion ranged widely. Although most of those present were still in their twenties or early thirties, there was a general feeling of despair about the 'younger generation'. Young men 'used to join the UDA …to go out and take the war to the Nationalist community'. Nowadays, if they joined, it was for 'the wrong reasons' – to get protection while paying off drug debts, for instance. Many kids nowadays were just 'interested in drugs and drink'. The question was raised – would the UDA be happy if the churches became more proactive in winning young people from a 'drug and drink' lifestyle and, as a result, recruitment to the UDA started to dry up? No clear answer was given to this question.

One senior UDA man from the town's Nelson Drive estate explained how if there was a 'party house' where carousing was going on till dawn, it 'certainly wouldn't be the police the neighbours would send for but …the local UDA chief' who would immediately send round a group of men to 'get it sorted out'. The opinion was generally expressed that 'all kinds of wee old ladies' looked to the UDA to 'handle the situation' and that even some 'church people' would be more than happy to see paramilitaries hand out a beating although they might 'tut-tut about it to their neighbours next day'.

One other UDA man said – somewhat surprisingly – that he had 'nothing against' a typical IRA man and in fact he would 'respect him for being prepared to fight and die for what he believed in.' Whereas the Republican combatant deserved some respect, there was a general perception that the police were 'merely doing their job for the money'. One man described the police as 'corrupt' and 'crooked' and cited the way in which he and his family had been 'harassed by the coppers'. [19]

A Biblical Rationale for Engaging with Militant Loyalism

Those clergy who work closely with paramilitaries have usually had to work out a biblical rationale for engagement. One such man, interviewed under conditions of anonymity, stresses that any engagement with militant Loyalism would be incomplete without stressing the political and social context in which

Christ found himself. He believes it was a political environment that bears some parallels with the one to be found in Ulster in recent times.

Palestine in that era began to seethe with deep discontent at the imperial rule of Rome. Resentment had been stoked by the census of AD 6, which was seen as a key bureaucratic part of an attempt to incorporate Judea into the provincial system of the Empire. Members of the Zealot movement, which flourished most effectively in the years after Christ's death, refused to pay taxes, objected to use of the Greek language, and refused to call Caesar 'Lord'. The Zealots would eventually resort to the harrying and murder of government officials, including those Jews whom they deemed to be 'collaborators'. There were widespread cases of killing involving 'dagger-men' who assassinated those whom they regarded as 'enemies of the nation' in a way that eerily foreshadows the clandestine planning and unforeseen targeting of modern terrorism.

In Jesus' day, Galilee, a deprived and relatively impoverished part of Judea, was the home to a number of gangs motivated by anti-Roman sentiment, which, in later years, would form the basis for the fully-formed Zealot movement. Jesus would certainly have been familiar with the resentment felt in many Galilean circles that the metropolitan elite in Jerusalem was selling out to Rome for privileges that the poor village-dwellers of Galilee could never experience. He would have known the arguments of those who believed that Roman institutions had to be attacked to prevent Jewish religion and culture being crushed. Equally, he must have recognised the deep challenge to that anti-imperial militancy which was presented by his practice of mingling with government tax-collectors and Roman centurions, as well as by teachings that stressed non-violence and the primal need for an inner, personal revolution.

Yet, arguably, Simon the Zealot who is mentioned in the list of the twelve disciples was – or had been – one such militant. If so, it seems that Christ was happy to include within his inner circle someone who might nowadays be termed a 'terrorist' – or at the very least an 'ex-combatant.'

Despite the non-violence of his message, Christ was clearly sufficiently associated with the threat of insurrection to be tried as a would-be 'King of the Jews' and subjected to the mode of execution usually reserved for political crimes – crucifixion. Undoubtedly then, the whole Jesus story is intermingled with narratives of regional and national identity, perceived under-privilege and political violence. The clergyman I interviewed reckons that any interpretation of the New Testament that fails to do justice to this fact has been sanitised. He believes such a sanitised interpretation is also impotent to speak into the life situation of those who have seen themselves as freedom-fighters in the recent Ulster conflict.

A Police Officer Speaks

Concluding this chapter, a police commander in one of Ulster's dominantly Protestant towns offers his opinions on the role of the Police Service which some UDA men seem to despise. Thomas Mahood is the officer in charge of the Police Station in Carrickfergus and was interviewed in November 2007:

> The reason why a number of local people always went to the paramilitaries to deal with their problems was because they got an immediate response. The paramilitary gang usually acted swiftly as jury, judge and – quite literally at times – as executioner. The police, on the other hand, always take time over a crime because a case has to be built up and legal process has to be gone through. Guilt has to be proven beyond reasonable doubt.
>
> We have indeed seen a reduction in the willingness of the paramilitaries to engage in punishments but this transformation has not always led to positive results as a number of criminals now see their way cleared to increase their activity. As a result, we have recently seen more burglaries in working-class areas in our district. The only ultimate solution is for the PSNI to become more and more involved in these communities.
>
> I would say that I have got some very good beat officers now involved in policing the Castlemara and Sunnylands estates. They are well respected and local people know that they can chat to them but also that they will be prepared to prosecute, if crimes are being committed. I would say that working-class communities, both Protestant and Catholic, are well represented in our police service. The majority of the policemen and policewomen who work for me here at the station are from a working-class background. And 38% of the workforce here lives in the Carrickfergus borough – that is in line with the recommendation by Patton that, where possible, communities should be policed by local people.
>
> I would say that we achieve a good response rate here – 90% of the emergency calls that we receive are answered within our target response time. There has been an increase in the amount of anti-social behaviour being dealt with by the police in the borough. However that is because we

are intervening more frequently and effectively, to nip trouble in the bud before it ends up with a case of criminal damage. Even during the recent feud between the rival elements in the UDA, I was still able to make sure that local everyday policing didn't suffer, because regional units were available to me, in order to help deal with these disturbances.

We have tried hard to create activities to keep the local youth engaged. In particular, during the past summer, we organised a midnight football league at the leisure centre, on Friday nights. We were anticipating 50 kids to turn up but in the end over 300 appeared. Now the council is thinking of organising a 'twilight' league on a more permanent basis. The Community Safety Unit here is very good. The officers would be on first name terms with many of the kids and they do a lot of work in local schools. This is one of several positive initiatives for which we have been responsible, including the creation of a local organisation to deal properly with the issue of domestic violence.

The UDA here now say that they have a two-year plan to 'go out of business'. Already there has been improvement in the area of what you might call extortion. This summer was the first in recent memory when businesses were not asked to "give donations", something that used to happen on a twice-yearly basis. I suppose the big worry is that the paramilitary structure will splinter amidst all of this and that criminal gangs will result, intent on keeping their members in the lifestyle to which they have become accustomed. A big advantage for me is that I grew up on the same estate as many of these guys and they know me well. My aim is to make this town a better and safer place for all its citizens and give something back to the place where I was born and grew up.

Yes, there is a place for churches to become more involved with the community. That would be positive. But it means, above all else, working with the young people, for they are the next generation. I am very grateful for the church on our estate whose youth facilities I availed of as a teenager. That helped keep me out of trouble and helped me along the road to where I am today.[20]

However, if Thomas Mahood is one of those working-class Protestants who succeeded in forging a police career, there are, as he indicates, many men from a similar background who followed an alternative trajectory on the civic margins, in the close-knit, dangerous and bloody world of armed Loyalism. There is something rather surprising – yet perhaps in the end appropriate – that one of the most articulate voices to advocate a new Christian approach to community engagement should come from these margins, in the shape of the high-ranking UVF ex-combatant, Billy Mitchell.

[1] Steve Bruce, *The Edge of the Union: Ulster Loyalist Political Vision*, (Oxford University Press, 1994) pp 1-2, p 30.

[2] Peter Shirlow and Mark McGovern eds., *Who Are The People? Unionism, Protestantism and Loyalism in Northern Ireland*, (Pluto Press, 1997) p 177.

[3] Brian Kennaway, *The Orange Order: A Tradition Betrayed* (Methuen, 2006) p 18.

[4] See article entitled 'Profile of the Orange Order,' 4 July 2000 at http://news.bbc.co.uk/1/hi/northern_ireland/1422212.stm. Accessed 20 August 2007.

[5] Interview with Rev Mervyn Gibson, Belfast, June 2007

[6] Information used here, including the quotation from ATQ Stewart, on Orange culture is carried on www.grandorange.org.uk. Accessed 2 June 2007.

[7] See www.grandorangelodge.co.uk/parades/marching_order.html and www.granorangelodge.co.uk/parades/traditions_parades.html. Accessed on 12 June 2007.

[8] Brian Kennaway, *The Orange Order: A Tradition Betrayed* (Methuen, 2006) p155. For information on the Whiterock disturbances see any Irish newspapers for September 2005

[9] For information on an attempt to redefine the relationship of the Church of Ireland and the Orange Order, see Earl Storey, *Traditional Roots: An Appropriate Relationship Between the Church of Ireland and the Orange Order* (Columba Press, 2002).

[10] Interview with a representative from Tyrone Orange Vision project, conducted in Belfast, November 2007.

[11] For this information on the history of the Ulster Volunteer Force see Jim Cusack and Henry McDonald, UVF, (Poolbeg Press, 1997).

[12] Information on the 'de-activation' of the UVF is found in Belfast Telegraph, 3 May 2007.

[13] Colin Crawford, *Inside the UDA: Volunteers and Violence* (Pluto Press, 2003) p 20.

[14] Colin Crawford, *Inside the UDA: Volunteers and Violence* (Pluto Press, 2003) p 42.

[15] Steve Bruce, *The Red Hand: Protestant Paramilitaries in Northern Ireland* (Oxford University Press, 1992) pp 227-237.

[16] Colin Crawford, *Inside the UDA: Volunteers and Violence* (Pluto Press, 2003) pp 61-62.

[17] Insights into ex-combatant perceptions of the church were obtained through conversations with Tom Roberts, the EPIC Centre, Woodvale, Belfast, June 2007.

[18] Information about his brother, who works in Japan, was given by George Brown, Newtownabbey.

[19] Interviews with UDA men in Derry, conducted November 2007.

[20] Interview with Inspector Thomas Mahood in Carrickfergus, conducted November 2007.

NEW LOYALTIES | 36

4 a voice from the margins

At Billy's Mitchell's funeral in 2006, numerous Republicans attended as well as several hundred Ulster Volunteer Force men. This wide mix of people bore witness to his cross-community profile. He had been an active figure in the UVF in the 1970s and was imprisoned in Long Kesh and Maghaberry gaols from 1976 until 1990. During 1979, he came to faith in Christ and found his life transformed.[1] At his funeral, one friend and Christian community worker spoke with warmth about Billy's positive impact:

> Many of us learned to walk this way by following him. We learned where to put our feet and where to tread lightly or stomp right in by watching and listening to him…Billy knew instinctively how to walk with people on their journey…he could stand alongside some of the people who are most reviled in our community yet they never felt judged by him… [2]

This chapter reveals how, from the time of his release until his untimely death, Billy worked hard as a political and community activist within the culture to which he still felt proud to belong. Billy felt that in this society, the dice was seriously loaded against working-class Loyalists right from the start of their lives and he called for local churches to 'show selfless, sacrificial solidarity' with these 'victims of structural injustice'.[3] His is a theology that evolved within a genuinely Loyalist working-class context and it deserves attention for that very reason.

A Paramilitary Career and a Christian Conversion

Billy Mitchell was born in 1940 in Ballyduff in County Antrim. His father died when he was two and the family moved a short distance to Glengormley where his mother worked in a mill and was a Sunday school teacher in the local Baptist church.[4] Billy would later reflect on his early upbringing and its significance:

> The home where I spent the bulk of my childhood was a wooden hut that has long since been demolished…there was no running water… a large bucket served as a toilet…for entertainment we had a wireless…for pets we had field mice…I was supposed to be one of the privileged prods [but] when I was in Long Kesh I encountered dozens upon dozens of Loyalists…whose experiences of growing up were similar to my own…we know from personal experience what it is like to live below the poverty line. Our upbringing made us practical social activists.[5]

Billy rejected the strict church upbringing to which his mother introduced him. His life as a teenager soon 'revolved around music, dances and girls'. But by the mid-1960s, he was an active Loyalist, playing in a flute band and joining an Orange Lodge. He and his friends went to hear Ian Paisley speak both at his church and at his famous Ulster Hall rallies and imbibed both the fundamentalist spirituality and the reactionary rhetoric. He then became involved with Paisley's Ulster Protestant Volunteers[6] but, as the Troubles began, joined the local unit of the more powerful and militant Ulster Volunteer Force. He rose quickly to the position of Commander of the East Antrim Battalion and membership of the central brigade staff.

Up until his arrest and sentencing for involvement in murder in 1976, Billy Mitchell was a committed and influential paramilitary. Through his role as editor of the UVF magazine, *Combat*, he had more space to reflect on political issues than the average Loyalist paramilitary leader. He was also very much involved in the IRA/UVF talks of 1974 – innovative discussions that were met with considerable hostility from suspicious fellow-Loyalists both inside and outside the UVF. At one stage Billy issued an appeal on behalf of the organisation which possessed a remarkably positive tone, calling 'on all Ulstermen to pause, to stretch out the hand of forbearance and conciliation, to forgive and forget, and to join in making for the province they love a new era of peace, contentment and goodwill' and suggesting the formation of a Council of Ulster under a neutral chair, with representations to be made by all sides of the community.

The progressive nature of the document led to accusations of treachery and the beginnings of a murderous feud. A 'supergrass' trial followed, involving the incrimination of numerous suspects by means of the testimony of a key informer, ending with long sentences being handed out to several UVF men, including Billy who, it would seem, did not pull a trigger during the feud but definitely shared in the guilt, in a way that he was later reluctant to discuss.[7] Billy was soon in prison, leaving behind his wife of five years and facing the prospect of 25 years' incarceration.

Prison was a hugely formative experience. Along with other notable UVF prisoners such as David Ervine and Billy Hutchinson, Billy Mitchell came under the influence of his commanding officer in gaol, Gusty Spence, who encouraged the men to read, to talk and to think deeply – especially about the reasons why they, as self-styled guardians of the state, had ended up behind bars. As Billy would later state 'That's what Long Kesh was all about. It was about investigating our backgrounds, our attitudes to life and everything else. The way people have been manipulated and told that they were "the people"'.

Billy read philosophers such as Sartre, political theorists such as Fanon, psychologists such as Frankl and novelists like Camus. Particularly after his conversion experience in 1979, he read theologians such as Karl Barth and investigated Christian thinkers and activists like FD Maurice, RH Tawney, George Lansbury and Keir Hardie. He found out all he could about radical, egalitarian reformation sects such as the Anabaptists and about modern-day church leaders who were also practitioners of a socially engaged faith such as Desmond Tutu and Oscar Arnulfo Romero. On Gusty Spence's express bidding Billy acquainted himself with the life and writings of Dietrich Bonhoeffer, whose sense of ethical commitment had led him to become involved in the plot to kill Hitler, for which he paid with his life.

Billy was also encouraged by his prison tutor to re-examine the Bible as an inspiring and diverse body of literature. In Billy's own words, his reading increasingly focused on 'stories about people of faith trying to make a difference' and writers who stressed that there must be 'social outcomes from Christian behaviour [and] social redemption'. The presence of Spence was very apparent during those Long Kesh years. On one occasion Spence told Billy, 'The sermon on the mount, that's what it's all about. You've got two coats, give one to your brother…that's the kind of Christianity I believe in.'[8] Billy would later reflect on the prison experience as a time when he at last learnt the importance of blending a benign political cause with a radical Christian faith. He would write that in his pre-prison years he had been, instead, merely 'a spiritual being who had been trying to satisfy…spiritual needs through political action'.[9]

Practical Peace-building in Loyalist Communities

Released in 1990, having served 14 years of his sentence, Billy Mitchell found domestic life outside gaol to be very difficult and he would later state 'I felt a stranger in my own house.' However, he soon threw himself into community work which focused on ex-prisoners, founding the LINC initiative – Local Initiatives for Needy Communities – under the auspices of the Church of the Nazarene, a small Evangelical denomination with a strong emphasis on compassionate, practical ministry. LINC offered vocational training to ex-prisoners and a number of art and craft workshops, run by Billy's wife, Mena. With the arrival of the Loyalist ceasefire in 1994, he also involved himself in the work of the Progressive Unionist Party, (PUP) which had a close relationship with the UVF. Some of his most important work involved the establishment of local 'conflict transformation' projects to regenerate Loyalist communities and to help educate Loyalist ex-combatants in a way of thinking that turned on the resolution of conflict through dialogue and community development rather than through violence. In this regard he was greatly helped by his friendship with the American Mennonite activist, John Paul Lederach, who had experience of conflict transformation processes in Nicaragua and Guatemala.

The writer Roy Garland was present at one such gathering of a Conflict Transformation initiative and was amazed by what he saw:

'We were deeply impressed and moved as young and older people, many of whom had never spoken publicly, delivered reports. Issues being addressed included a Young Citizens' Forum, flags, sectarianism, murals and bonfires. Others ranged from hockey, soccer coaching and fitness training to community safety, senior citizens, anti-social behaviour, heritage, cultural and historical interests, outdoor pursuits with police, projects to tidy and enhance areas, youth painting projects, drugs awareness, employment skills, child protection, women's groups, first aid, food hygiene, home safety, cancer awareness, beauty treatment, neighbourhood mediation, cross-border relationships, mediation leadership training, team building, information sessions with the Police Ombudsman, human rights, a community garden, citizens' advice, healthy living, fuel poverty, codes of conduct for bands and much more besides. I was astounded. I had never before witnessed anything so constructive and visionary being undertaken by any political party on such a scale and there in the centre sat Billy Mitchell. He had defied the inertia, pessimism, sectarianism and class division that for so long have bedevilled this community.'[10]

Billy also contributed to practical peace-building through the instigation of restorative justice projects, centring on an attempt to bring perpetrator and victim together in a way that effects reparation and res-olution for the victim and repentance and reform on the part of the perpetrator, with the needs of the community also being paramount. He saw that the contract between the perpetrator and the victim would ideally involve 'regret expressed and recompense agreed' and that this kind of agreement was in keeping with the Old Testament principle of 'an eye for an eye, a tooth for a tooth' – a notion which, rather than enacting sterile vengeance, as is too often suggested, could act as a means of placing equable, measured recompense at the heart of the system of justice.

Through the influence of Billy and a number of other people in the UVF/PUP grouping, the so-called 'Alternatives' project – noted in the previous chapter – was pioneered in order to further the use of restorative justice in Loyalist communities whereby victim-offender mediation could become the nor-mative way of dealing with petty crime and anti-social behaviour rather than the 'traditional' methods of punishment beatings and expulsions from the offender's host community. Despite remarkable successes, as validated by authoritative external observers, the project has faced all kinds of obstacles, not least the widespread public feeling that restorative justice subverts the rule of the law and legitimate policing and is another form of paramilitary control. This is something which Billy always endeavoured to refute:

> Restorative justice is a non-violent and non-coercive response to socially harmful activity. Individ-uals participate on a voluntary basis only and none of our programmes support coercion, impose sanctions, physical pain or expulsion. The ultimate goal is …to help create safer communities.[11]

Billy was committed to the idea that focus on non-violent resolution could also work in the larger political arena where Northern Ireland's 'two communities' play out their destinies. The process of reconciliation and mutual understanding should involve ex-prisoners, like himself. As he told the writer Kate Fearon:

> Peace-building is about seeking a commitment to developing creative alternatives to violence through dialogue with the enemy [and] current and former participants in the conflict are a key resource in the peace-building process…they must however be sincere in their desire for both non-violence and the democratic process.[12]

A Theology that Makes Sense for Working-class Loyalism?

Billy Mitchell worked out a Christian philosophy that dovetailed with his activism. One thing that he stressed as absolutely vital in Ulster was the Christian imperative to effect reconciliation through for-giveness. In one of his *Conflict Transformation Papers* he quoted the utterance of the suffering Christ in Luke 23, 'Father, forgive them; for they know not what they are doing…' He then went on to suggest, in the light of this divine example, that in Northern Ireland 'the power and excellence of true Christianity is its propensity to dispose us to pray for the forgiveness of our enemies.'[13]

Reading Scripture in the troubled and broken context of the society in which he found himself, Billy referred to the killing of Stephen the martyr, in starkly Northern Irish terms as a 'brutal sectarian murder.' Yet in the midst of being killed by his enemies Stephen had found the God-given strength to call out 'Lord do not hold this sin against them.'[14] In the same Conflict Transformation Paper, Billy went on to refer to the beating and humiliation of Jesus in Ulster parlance as 'the greatest punishment beating that ever took place', yet one which did not prevent Christ from seeking God's forgiveness for the gang who attacked him. Of crucial importance, Billy suggested, were examples of forgiveness in action in Ulster society

such as Gordon Wilson, who spoke of his immediate forgiveness of the IRA bombers who killed his daughter in the Enniskillen 'Poppy Day Bomb'. For Billy the words of Martin Luther King Jr were inspirational and he quoted with approval a passage from King's book *Strength to Love*, where the famous civil rights activist gives advice that 'returning hate for hate multiplies hate, adding deeper darkness to a night already devoid of stars.'

In evolving this localised theology of forgiveness and reconciliation, Billy found Galatians 6 to be another key text, where Paul says 'May I never boast of anything except the cross of our Lord Jesus Christ by which the world has been crucified to me and I to the world.' For Billy, the cross was central to Christian thinking because it showed God's total identification with human suffering and his desire and power to reconcile broken humanity to himself. The cross, to Billy, showed the nature of genuine restorative justice: 'men see justice purely in terms of retribution…God sees justice as a means of restoring broken relationships and establishing just relationships…' Billy felt that it was his own duty, in turn, to live out that reconciliatory story of the cross in his daily life 'The task of working for reconciliation…is not an option for me… it is a divine command [and] I attribute the change in my life…to the transforming power of the cross.'[15]

Another crucial text in Billy's thinking was 1 Peter 3, where the biblical author refers to the period between Christ's death and resurrection as the time when 'He went and made a proclamation to the spirits in prison' – a passage usually interpreted as being about Christ's descent into hell, in order to reach those who were imprisoned there with his saving power. This text emphasised for Billy the depth to which Jesus was prepared to go to reach the condemned, the trapped and the lost. It set the standard for the church, which ought therefore to be 'embracing and experiencing the struggle of the dispossessed and the disempowered' here in Ulster society, in which Christians must 'show selfless, sacrificial solidarity' with those who are suffering, who are abandoned, hopeless or rejected.

Because 'the victory over death and Hell and evil was…won on Holy Saturday in the dark and hostile caverns of the underworld…' the Church must surely recognise its role as a rescuer of those who are caught in the darkest and most abandoned corners of society – 'in the world of injustice where prejudice, intolerance, exploitation and violence hold their prey in a vice-like grip…that is where Christians ought to be…'[16]

He relished the example of the martyred Archbishop of San Salvador, Oscar Arnulfo Romero, an exponent of non-violent Liberation Theology, as someone who put his Christ-like love for the poor and needy to the ultimate test:

> Wherever men and women suffer injustice, Christ is crucified afresh, for He is there in the midst of them. The people's bishop, Arnulfo Romero, saw the crucified God in the midst of the crucified men and women of history. In the faces of the poor and oppressed of El Salvador he saw the disfigured face of God. It was that vision of the Crucified in the midst of His suffering people that inspired Archbishop Romero to enter into solidarity with both their sufferings and their struggle. It cost Romero his life – that too can be the cost of following Christ. [17]

To Billy it seemed clear that the violence in Northern Ireland had helped create vast untreated areas of social need, particularly in the numerous partisan ghettoes of the province. Unfortunately the traditional church had been 'locked away in their holy huddles and spiritual bunkers' and had 'lost the significance of the incarnational theology' touched on by Paul in Philippians 2, where Christ is said to have 'emptied himself, taking the form of a slave, being born in human likeness…'

Rather than coming to terms with its own failure over the years to 'build a bridge between a world of hurting humanity and the love and compassion of a healing Saviour', the middle-class church had used paramilitaries as a scapegoat to blame for the violence in Northern Ireland. By so-doing the church had covered its own inadequacies and indeed its own complicity in prejudice and its half-hidden pleasure at reprisal. 'In Northern Ireland we have ready-made scapegoats in the paramilitaries…so long as we can point to the scapegoat, we have no need to look at ourselves.'

Clearly, because of his own personal experiences, Billy had been sensitised to the plight of all former Loyalist 'activists' who found a 'respectable' Protestant community turning its back on those who had committed murders and suffered incarceration in that community's name and having been inspired by one of that community's firebrand leaders. For him, it was important that middle-class Ulster Protestants recognise that the Loyalist paramilitaries 'are not animals like the Hebrew scapegoat…they are flesh of our flesh and bone of our bone. They are the manifestation of our failure to resolve our difficulties…'

A Place of Injustice is Where Christians Ought to Be

For Billy, the role of all believers had to be centred on the teaching found in Matthew 5, where Christ speaks of his followers as being 'the salt of the earth' and 'the light of the world'. As a self-styled 'Christian community activist' Billy felt it was his duty to busy himself in his own community 'preserving society from corruption' and 'shedding light on all aspects of human darkness'. He indicated on several occasions that he saw Jesus as a man with a 'passion for transforming social structures' and that that divine ministry on earth had indicated 'a special place in the heart of God for the poor'. Billy went on to spell out that 'Christ's great work was…to remove the causes which divided man from man, to make it impossible for the strong to oppress the weak or the rich to rob the poor.'

In light of the fact that Jesus' mission was focused on the distressed and disadvantaged, Billy often wrote with passion and distress about the way that marginalised working-class Protestants in Northern Ireland often felt that the 'mainstream churches have opted out of local community life' in their areas, while 'the smaller evangelical churches', who often stayed physically present on working-class sites, were 'so heavenly-minded that they have lost touch with many of the harsh realities of life on earth.'[18] It was now crucial, in Billy Mitchell's eyes, for Ulster's Evangelical Christians to see that 'Christianity is social and personal' and that 'they ought to work for the enrichment and enhancement of life and to combat those social evils that lead to deprivation, alienation, conflict and violence…' The local Evangelical churches badly needed a leadership that understood the importance of both evangelistic and social gospels and he lamented the fact that 'community development is not a concept that is taught at theological seminary or that is included in the curriculum of Christian training colleges.' Community-development training should focus on churches finding out what local, underprivileged communities felt they needed and then seeing what they could do to meet those needs.

That training also ought to clarify and broaden the Northern Irish Protestant sense of what sin actually is 'If sin is to be denounced, it must not be restricted to the usual personal failures associated with drink, gambling, fornication and crime. It must also include those corporate sins that are responsible for structural violence – economic greed, political exploitation, de-socialisation, disculturation, racism and sectarianism.'[19]

It was thus important, in his eyes, that all Christian intellectuals, including theologians, speak up on issues of social justice, rather than remain in their theoretical ivory towers. In this respect, he was happy to quote Noam Chomsky's statement that 'it is the responsibility of intellectuals to speak the truth and expose lies'.[20]

One of the key elements in Billy's whole project was the attempt to place Protestant, Unionist and Loyalist cultures on a surer, more ideologically aspirational footing. This was a task rendered all the more difficult by the political sterility in Unionist ranks and the descent into unashamed criminality among a number of Loyalists. In the ground-breaking magazine *The Other View*, which Billy and some Loyalist friends jointly edited with men from a Republican background, he set out his cultural loyalties clearly, along with their democratic implication: 'Following the dissenting tradition of the Scotch-Irish community… I am diametrically opposed to any form of government where absolute power is held by any individuals who are not accountable to the people…'[21]

In an article called 'In defence of the Faith', Billy's mind was focused upon the inappropriateness of creating a Protestant ascendancy despite the value of having Reformed Christian moral values informing one's politics. He wrote that 'Unionists must accept the multi-faith and multi-cultural nature of the United Kingdom…there is no room in a pluralist society for a State Church.' He went on to assert that 'we, as Protestants, must reject any alliance between church and state and any reliance upon political parties to legislate in defence of our faith.' Loyalism therefore ought to be focused on seeing 'full and equal citizenship within a multi-faith and multi-cultural Union'. Loyalists also ought to be committed to 'a classless society where all citizens are afforded equality in terms of…race, religion, gender, sexual orientation, age, [and] disability…' This would be a Loyalism of plurality, which sees only Christ and his followers – and not politicians or paramilitaries – as defenders of the Protestant faith. It would be a Loyalism 'true to the legacy of the Reformation.'

Looking Again at the Ulster Covenant

In trying to provide this surer, more positive footing, Billy Mitchell spent time endeavouring to bring Ulster Loyalists back to the founding document of Northern Irish Unionism, the Ulster Covenant of 1912, which he believed held a number of ideals which were capable of filling the ideological void in working-class Protestant areas. These ideals, as espoused by Billy on the website of the Progressive Unionist Party, included an emphasis on seeking the material well-being of Ulster as part of the United Kingdom, equal citizenship for all Ulstermen and women within the United Kingdom, civic and religious freedom for all who were resident within Ulster's boundaries and finally – and most controversially – the right of armed resistance against those deemed to be posing a threat to the democratic wishes of the Ulster people.

We can see here a real tension in Billy's work. He repeatedly promoted the Christian ethic of reconciliation and the benefit of non-violent solutions throughout his post-prison career. Nonetheless, he felt compelled at times to articulate the moral case for a threatened people resorting to the gun when ultimately required, as many Loyalists had once believed they had to do, here in Northern Ireland.

In a document that may have been aimed at an internal UVF readership in a time of change, re-evaluation and increased politicisation, Billy looked back at the period of the UVF 'terrorist' campaign from 1970 to 1994 and suggested to his readers that, in the face of the IRA campaign of violence, the Ulster Volunteer Force felt that 'effective resistance within the Rule of Law was impossible'. The IRA was, after all, an 'invisible army', mingling with and obtaining considerable support from the Nationalist population. He reminded his readers that 'the IRA did not wear easily recognisable uniforms and did not operate foot patrols or tour the streets of our cities and villages in easily identifiable vehicles.' Whereas the IRA could operate a campaign of ambushes against the highly visible forces of the state, any attempt by the army or the police to copy the terrorist strategy and ambush IRA men, always met with international condemnation. In other words, 'the rules of engagement must always favour the IRA and other anti-state groups.'

Billy suggested that it was in this specific military context that UVF leaders of the day made the conscious decision to operate a counter-terrorist campaign, which would fight a war against 'the community that gave birth to and nurtured the IRA.' He mentioned how numerous key UVF figures were ex-British Army men with an experience of the cruel realities of counter-terrorism in Cyprus and Malaya. They understood the need for a 'harsh and ruthless strategy' that was 'dictated by the nature of the conflict', in which the Catholic people were '…the only visible enemy that could be targeted.' In this sense, Billy argued, 'the IRA invited reprisal attacks against the Nationalist community.'

This analysis sounds like an apologia for a campaign of bombs and assassinations that at the time seemed more motivated by blind anger than cool strategy. It seems to sit at odds with Billy's public advocacy of non-violent solutions to community conflicts. He added to it by suggesting that the heavy attrition rate in terms of Catholic casualties was a key factor in bringing the IRA to the conference table

and thus to the evolution of the entire peace process. He then drew attention to the fact that 'the use of terror tactics in conflict has never been restricted to "terrorist" organisations and lest anyone should hasten to morally distance themselves from this UVF rationale for targeting Catholic civilians, he dwelt on the fact that the now globally revered war against fascism 1939-1945 was often conducted against civilian targets and that 'the carpet-bombing of German towns by RAF bomber command under Arthur 'Bomber' Harris and the total destruction of Hiroshima and Nagasaki by the United States Air Force were all designed to terrorise the enemy.'

Billy Mitchell's explanation for the targeting of civilians was possibly not just aimed at an internal readership, but at a wider non-paramilitary audience who were thinking of affiliating themselves to the left-of-centre PUP enterprise. Possibly it was an attempt to help these potential supporters perceive, though not to endorse, the thinking process behind the often-ruthless actions of the Loyalist combatants.

Arguably, these combatants have too-often been labelled as animalistic sectarian killers and precious few attempts such as Billy's have been made to interpret their motivations and strategies compared with Republican volunteers, in whose campaigns civilians were also frequent victims. The widely understood ethos of a national liberation movement has often been readily employed to give the IRA's struggle moral high ground and their members the status of soldiers, despite much resultant carnage. Billy Mitchell's argument can perhaps be seen as an attempt to re-imagine a military rationale for the Loyalist gunman – but arguably only in order to recognise in his capacity for killing 'soft targets' an all too prevalent feature of the inhumane art of war.

In this chapter it has been important to major on Billy's role as Christian peacemaker, which he undoubtedly fulfilled with resolution, insight and courage. However, he also occupied the role of UVF veteran and Progressive Unionist Party mentor who felt the need to explain and offer a logic, within the charged, chaotic context of the Troubles, for a Loyalist espousal of violence. Possibly, without playing this role he would not have had the influence that he came to exert in militant Loyalist circles during the Peace Process.

As has already been stressed, those who involve themselves more fully with marginalised communities where Loyalist paramilitaries are held in esteem will have to face up to a number of uncomfortable facts. For one thing, innovative and authentic theology can be generated in a UVF prison cell as readily as in a professional theologian's study. Secondly, panic and barbarism can befall an ordinary community, in which men and women of considerable conviction and humanity make choices that lead to the imposition of further violence and suffering that we have come to know as 'terrorism'. Involvement with Loyalist communities will lead to many such uncomfortable insights into the complex moral realities and deeply brutal outcomes of civil conflict, which have been all too easy to ignore in many middle-class drawing-rooms in Unionist Ulster.

[1] This information comes from a set of essays written by Roy Garland exploring Billy Mitchell's legacy in *The Irish News*, 31 July 2006 and 4 September 2006 and in Corrymeela magazine, volume 6, issue 3, p 16-17.

[2] Extracts are taken from the script of a funeral address by Glenn Jordan, loaned to the author by the speaker.

[3] Billy Mitchell, 'Community Development and the Churches' in *Conflict Transformation Papers, Volume 6: Faith, Politics and Social Action*, located at www.linc-ncm.org/CTP_6.PDF. Accessed 7 May 2007.

[4] Kate Fearon, *The Conflict's Fifth Business: A Brief Biography of Billy Mitchell*, www.linc.ncm.org/No.2.PDF. Accessed 9-10 May 2007.

[5] Billy Mitchell 'The Privileged Prod and the Travelling Tinker', *The Other View*, Issue 5, (Summer 2001) p. 2.

[6] Information is taken here from a set of essays on the legacy of Billy Mitchell, written by Roy Garland in *The Irish News*, 31 July 2006 and 4 September 2006 and in *Corrymeela* magazine, Volume 6, issue 3, p 16-17.

[7] Information is taken here from a set of essays on the legacy of Billy Mitchell, written by Roy Garland in The Irish News, 31 July 2006 and 4 September 2006 and in Corrymeela magazine, Volume 6, issue 3, p 16-17.

[8] Kate Fearon, *The Conflict's Fifth Business: A Brief Biography of Billy Mitchell*, www.linc.ncm.org/nO.2.PDF. Accessed 8-10 May 2007

[9] Information on Billy Mitchell's life and work was carried at www.sundsgarden.nu/eri. Accessed 5 May 2007.

[10] Information is taken from a set of essays written on the legacy of Billy Mitchell, written by Roy Garland in *The Irish News*, 31 July 2006 and 4 September 2006 and in *Corrymeela* magazine, Volume 6, issue 3, pp 16-17.

[11] Billy Mitchell, 'Dealing with Socially Harmful Activities', *Conflict Transformation Papers*, *Volume 6*, Faith, Politics and Social Action, www.linc-ncm.org/CTP_6.PDF. Accessed 18 May 2007.

[12] Kate Fearon, *The Conflict's Fifth Business: A Brief Biography of Billy Mitchell*, www.linc.ncm.org/No.2.PDF. Accessed 8-10 May 2007.

[13] Billy Mitchell, 'Father Forgive Them', *Conflict Transformation Papers*, Volume 6, Faith, Politics and Social Action, www.linc-ncm.org/CTP_6.PDF. Accessed 18 May 2007.

[14] Billy Mitchell, 'Father Forgive Them', *Conflict Transformation Papers*, Volume 6, Faith, Politics and Social Action, www.linc-ncm.org/CTP_6.PDF. Accessed 18 May 2007.

[15] Billy Mitchell, 'Glorying in the Cross' *Conflict Transformation Papers*, Volume 6, Faith, Politics and Social Action, www.linc-ncm.org/CTP_6.PDF Accessed 25 May 2007.

[16] Billy Mitchell, 'Liberating the Dead' (Reflection on Easter Saturday), *Conflict Transformation Papers*, Volume 6, Faith, Politics and Social Action, www.linc-ncm.org/CTP_6.PDF. Accessed 25 May 2007.

[17] Billy Mitchell, 'Liberating the Dead' (Reflection on Easter Saturday), *Conflict Transformation Papers*, Volume 6, Faith, Politics and Social Action, www.linc-ncm.org/CTP_6.PDF. Accessed 25 May 2007.

[18] Billy Mitchell, *Conflict Transformation Papers*, Volume 6, Faith Politics and Social Action, www.linc-ncm.org/CTP_6.PDF. Accessed 25 May 2007, p 3.

[19] Billy Mitchell, 'Community Development and the Churches' in *Conflict Transformation Papers*, Volume 6: Faith, Politics and Social Action, www.linc-ncm.org/CTP_6.PDF. Accessed 25 May 2007.

[20] Billy Mitchell, 'In Defence of the Faith' in *Conflict Transformation Papers*, Volume 6: Faith, Politics and Social Action, www.linc-ncm.org/CTP_6.PDF. Accessed 25 May 2007.

[21] Billy Mitchell, 'The Monarchy' *The Other View*, Issue 1, (Spring 2000) p 1.x

[22] Billy Mitchell's article on the 'Principles of Loyalism' is carried on the website of the Progressive Unionist Party, www.pup-ni.org/loyalism/principlesdocument.asp.x. Accessed on 20 May 2007.

5

a global story?

This chapter attempts to show that the struggling communities in Protestant working-class areas of Northern Ireland are not unique. A few examples taken from England, the Republic of Ireland and the USA will confirm that Ulster's Loyalists are not endowed with a 'worst case' series of social difficulties. There will also be a close examination of Christian community work in 'challenging' locations within England and the USA, to see what can be learnt from their experience.

The chapter shows that global trends, which bring about both distress and social enrichment, play a role in the life of the province, as well as local factors. As this region opens to the outside world in the 'post-Troubles era', these trends will become increasingly important and no local community worker wishing to understand social dysfunction should ignore the possibility that the problems he or she witnesses are widely experienced elsewhere or have their origins far beyond the borders of Northern Ireland. Equally, no community worker, Christian or otherwise, should ignore the possibility that wisdom gained elsewhere is highly applicable here.

Deprivation and Despair Despite the Celtic Tiger

In the Republic of Ireland, housing estates in cities such as Dublin and Limerick continue to present massive problems despite the prosperity brought by the 'Celtic Tiger'. One community worker in a notorious Dublin estate, interviewed in January 2008, spoke of difficulties that have not been solved by a recent government-led regeneration scheme, which he feels may have concentrated too much on simply changing the physical infrastructure. Working particularly with men in the estate, he keeps on encountering groups of young males who are 'hacked off' by life and are often consumed with rage and destructiveness. Illustrative of this was a recent incident in which a group of teenage boys broke into the local community centre and, with much amusement, urinated over some Christmas party-packs that had been prepared for younger children in the area.

Frequently, he has witnessed older men failing to complete training courses that require a good attendance record and compliance with rules, deadlines and programmes of study. He suggests that there is a kind of male psyche that enjoys challenge, group identity, physicality, rebellion and risk, but simply cannot comply with the standards of propriety and intellect expected of a typical Irish job trainee. He can therefore readily understand why the dressed-up militarism of the Loyalist marching band and the camaraderie of the paramilitary drinking club are so important to young Ulster Protestant males.

As far as policing goes, it appears to be common knowledge that large parts of this Dublin estate are 'no-go' areas for the Gardai. It is common practice for local people to avoid being seen talking to a police officer in case the assumption is made that they are 'a tout'. In the absence of effective policing, every door and window in the community centre where he works has to be fitted with heavy-duty steel locks and shutters so as to avoid the premises being entered and 'trashed'. In the view of this one Irish community worker, the problems of male behaviour in tough urban environments are probably much the same every-where in the western world. He speculates that the only probable difference between the anti-social young man in Dublin and Belfast is the colour of his football shirt.[1]

What my interviewee might have added to the toxic mix, whether in Belfast or Dublin, is the prevailing postmodern environment, in which the grand, inspiring narratives have all disappeared. This is a world permeated by consumption and ruled by round-the-clock access to television, video, internet, and mobile phone usage. Arguably this is a place where the questing spirit of the young male is the most vulnerable and the first to suffer anomie or bitter frustration, whether in Belfast or Dublin or anywhere else.

Disadvantage in English and American Society

Alongside its stockbroker belts and pretty rural villages, England possesses vast areas where ill health and educational failure are pervasive. The writer Lynsey Hanley, who grew up on a council state in Solihull, asserts that, in 2001, in Solihull a man could expect to live to 71 years and a woman to 77. However, within her estate the figures were 61 and 66 respectively. Communal ill health has many causes, not least a poor environment. She castigates the planners who built such estates according to inhumane architectural principles. She also blames the obsessive governmental ethos of home ownership for the depressed morale of the inhabitants and the sense of being at the 'bottom of the pile'.

She refers to the grim fact that those who grow up on English estates have a 10-15% chance of leaving school without any qualifications whatsoever and, at best, only 25-30% of them have a chance of getting the five good grades at GCSE that will be the minimum needed for any skilled job. She concludes that 'Estates are like ghettoes, in the sense that…they may as well have walls built around them… Estates are class ghettoes, places where few middle-class people aside from those who are paid to do so ever venture.'[2] Sadly, recent evidence suggests that in England the gap between the educational achievement levels of the rich and the poor is widening. As a result, students in leafy South Buckinghamshire are now 43% more likely to achieve five good GCSEs than students in the multi-racial, working-class London borough of Tower Hamlets.[3]

Nor should it be forgotten that the United States of America – arguably the world's most powerful country – possesses an underclass that struggles to survive in a society which too often regards poverty as moral failure. This is a group whose plight is often magnified by a sense of racial disadvantage, by a vicious gang and gun culture and a drug menace of epic proportions. There is also the vulnerability created by a system of medical care that is not free at point of need. One Christian community worker who receives help from the USA with his own project in North Belfast has spoken to me with amusement about the ironies of hearing well-intentioned American philanthropists ask him if they should send over consignments of medical equipment and medicines to Ulster, not realising that the British National Health Service, for all its many failings, provides the kind of free care about which many of the poorer citizens of the US can only dream.

So Northern Ireland's Protestant working-class communities face many of the social problems that have to be dealt with by similar communities elsewhere – and compared with some struggling groups in other western societies, they may actually possess comparative advantages. Nor should it be forgotten that compared with life in the slums of the mega-cities in the 'developing world', existence in the Belfast's Shankill or Derry's Waterside looks relatively idyllic.

Christian Community Life in a Deprived Part of London

The social challenges of Loyalist working-class areas are at least mitigated by the fact that people speak the same language and by and large share the same values. In the vast city of London a wide range of cultures share the same spaces and huge social fault-lines often exist. This is especially true of the Borough of Newham. It is probably the most ethnically mixed part of the capital, in which more than 100 languages are spoken amongst its quarter of a million inhabitants. In the summer of 2007 it was hosting over 400 refugees and asylum seekers. Only 39% of the population of Newham was registered as 'white' in 2004 with 32% registered as 'Asian' and 21% as 'Black'. In terms of religious affiliation, 46% described themselves as 'Christian' while 24% were 'Islamic', 7% 'Hindu' and 3% 'Sikh'. Despite ongoing attempts to rejuvenate the area, Newham still finds itself figuring on lists of British poverty and deprivation, being the fourth most deprived borough in London and the eleventh most deprived nationally. In 2007, a remarkable mix of more than 300 faith-based organisations existed in the borough, covering all the major world religions from Buddhism to Judaism, as well as smaller faiths such as Mormonism and Bahai.[4]

Many committed Christians in the area seem to be thriving on challenge rather than perishing within this inner urban context that is a kaleidoscope of poverty, multiple ethnicity, religious diversity and secularism. The organisation called 'Transform Newham' is made up of over 50 local churches whose leaders and congregations come together for regular prayer events, believing that – as their website puts it 'There is a new call of God for us to pray as one church…' and a need for 'repenting and being reconciled to past differences…' The emphasis is not just on corporate prayer but on 'Lighthouses of prayer' – individuals who agree to 'pray for their neighbours and/or their work colleagues'. There is also a strong emphasis on home-to-home visits in the borough, when Christian literature is offered to the householder.

However, the churches involved in this project also take the social commitment of the gospel very seriously. The organisation gives pride of place to the work of 'unity and reconciliation…crossing all cultures and denominations', recognising that all such reconciliation is 'in the heart of God.' To that end, the

Transform Newham website is packed with stories about local events that straddle racial and cultural divides such as the 'Positively Jamaica' festival, held in early August 2007, which celebrated the 45 years of Jamaican independence and was predominantly organised by local Christians and Christian Aid. There was a showcase of West Indian music, dance, poetry and food but also considerable emphasis on the work to combat HIV/Aids on the island, in a presentation given by a team from Christian Aid.

Also featured on the website is a recent BBC Radio report on the way in which Newham churches have been 'engaging with people of other faiths and working to meet the various needs of the residents in different ways.' The article focused on 'dead-end' kids whose lives had been turned around by a football academy started by the Plaistow 'Glory House' church. The youngsters in the nearby trouble-torn estate who attend the academy include Muslims, Hindus, Christians, some of other faiths and many of none. The radio article also dwelt on the work of the Alternative Crisis Pregnancy Centre, run by the Memorial Community Church in Plaistow. The centre attempts to help young women to find alternatives to abortion and about 200 clients a month are assisted there. The numbers so far have included over 60 nationalities and faith groups. As one centre worker told the journalist 'Churches in Newham have a real heart to engage with women of other faiths and we're keen to network as widely as we can in the community.'

Also reported by the BBC was the work of a church in Forest Gate which had organised a 'Stop Da Violence' concert, where music was interwoven with presentations focused on the battle against gun and knife-crime in the east end of London. One particularly innovative feature of Christian social witness in the borough – which the BBC did not cover – is the work of 'Street Pastors', visible Christian citizens who patrol the streets at night, seeking to establish a responsible adult presence, monitor trouble, offer help and defuse confrontations.

However, as other articles on the Transform Newham website show, Christian churches in the area also involve themselves in more controversial social and cultural issues. One article deals with opposition to the proposed establishment of a casino in the borough. It is a step seen by many Christians as an enticement into indebtedness in a part of London already suffering from more than its fair share of poverty. Another part of the site is devoted to a discussion of a highly sensitive issue – the proposed erection of a huge new mosque in the borough, a building project reportedly associated with the devout, expansionist Islamic group known as 'Tablighi Jamaat'. Quite clearly, Christians in Newham are caught in a difficult position. Though loath to see the Islamic presence in their neighbourhood augmented by such a 'showpiece', they neither want to offend the sensibilities of Islamic fellow-citizens nor be seen as allying themselves with the British National Party whose 'Jihad Watch' involves fierce denunciation of the Newham mosque project.[5]

As we look at the position of committed Christians in deeply multi-cultural environments such as Newham, it is apparent that such a setting need not hold back local believers, rather it may push them in the direction of co-operation and into a recognition of the value of vibrant, sensitive community work. Even so, there remain many challenges for the culturally sensitive Christian who may wish to retain good relations with non-Christian neighbours yet is concerned not to facilitate the growth of militant versions of rival faiths.

Bonny Downs Church – Community Work in a Deprived Multi-Cultural Setting

A brief examination of one Evangelical church in Newham vividly reveals some of the dynamics of Christian community involvement in an area of ethnic diversity, poverty and recent cultural change. It may also serve simply as an example of Evangelical social commitment in an area of struggle and alienation, which may offer learning for the Northern Ireland context.

Bonny Downs Baptist Church was founded in 1908 and meets in the Flanders Road area of the borough. In the summer of 2007 it had 200 'attenders', including 100 members. In its Edwardian heyday the church had a white working-class base but in multi-racial Newham it now has a truly 'global' congregation, in which a number of Nigerian and Angolan believers have been elected as deacons.

Eight years ago, the church moved its main work and worship into a nearby disused community centre but the old church building is still used for a range of supplementary meetings. There is talk of a new 'church plant' soon to be established in another community centre close by. The Bonny Downs Community Association was formed by church members in 1998 to begin the task of re-establishing the local community centre as a Christian base. Then in 2001, it was reopened under the new name of 'The Well', following an extensive refurbishment project in financial partnership with the borough authorities. The Well, which now has 1000 users a week, possesses a large hall, a number of children's areas, a workshop, offices, training and education rooms and a useful basement. There is an 'elders' project' on the site that cares for some of the older residents of East Ham and the Association owns the 'Flanders Field' nine-acre sports field nearby which has a number of fitness and sports projects connected to it. There is a range of family and childcare initiatives, a toy library for young children and courses aimed at local people with special needs and those who would like to gain better parenting skills. A host of volunteering opportunities are also on offer.

The community café offers good food at reasonable prices and internet access and a weekly advice and counselling facility provides help sorting out difficulties with welfare, benefits and pensions. The Association also manages a number of rooms on behalf of local landlords, in order to provide good quality housing for single people who are in education or training, those working in key professions such as nursing or teaching or who are endeavouring to survive on a low or reduced income. Such a strategy helps to contribute to the social capital of the neighbourhood and assists people at risk of falling to the very bottom of the housing ladder.

The Association's Flanders Field sports centre has received a substantial grant of £350,000, as part of the government's 'Sport England' project, to enable the Bonny Downs group to provide sport and recreation for local people, particularly among the under-represented and vulnerable sections of the community, including young people, women and girls, people on low incomes, minority ethnic groups, people with disabilities and older people. This is a classic example of a faith-based group taking full advantage of the modern opportunity to access public funds in order to provide a high-standard community service that promotes the well-being of the people and in doing so spreads the values of the kingdom of God.

Its literature and website state that the church's Community Association shares a 'common vision', motivated by their faith, which envisages both changed lives and a transformed community. While the mission and ethos of the Bonny Downs church itself is not only Christian in its principles but evangelistic in outreach, the Community Association has been endowed with a more communitarian vision, stating that it aims to 'work with people and organisations, regardless of their faith, towards a whole community, by providing excellent services and facilities that promote well-being, hope, opportunity, love and encouragement.' The Association declares its allegiance to the Faithworks Charter for faith-based community work, promising to 'serve and respect all peoples, regardless of their gender, marital status, race, ethnic origin, religion, age, sexual orientation or physical and mental capacity' and 'to develop partnerships with other churches, voluntary groups, statutory agencies and local government…to create an effective, integrated service for our clients.'

The Association also pledges 'never to impose our Christian faith and belief on others.' On the other hand, it does nail its colours to the mast as an organisation that subscribes to the Evangelical Alliance's Statement of Faith, centred on Trinitarian, Bible-centred Protestantism. It may be assumed that the Christian workers in the Association do therefore inhabit the place of tension that we have touched on in earlier chapters of this survey, between doing community work 'for its own sake' and doing it as a clear means of spreading the influence of the Christian faith.

Certainly the Bonny Downs church itself continues to thrive as a place of Christian worship and witness. The main morning service is now held in The Well community centre with refreshments served in the café for half an hour before the meeting begins. Nine small home groups also meet through the week as an extension of Christian fellowship and church members can engage in other valuable activities such as Monday's book discussion club, the regular arts and craft group – involving needlework, calligraphy and painting – and the 'All Age' coffee morning, held every Tuesday. Regular intercessory prayer for local politicians and leaders and 'prayer walks' on key roads in the district feature among the church's prayer activities.[6]

A London-Based Community Worker Speaks

Colin Marchant is a member of Bonny Downs Baptist Church. Now retired from full-time Christian work, for many years he was involved as a Baptist Pastor in church-based community work both in London and other parts of England. For Colin the Bonny Downs social projects and the larger story of the Transform Newham initiative have been deeply inspiring. His advice to those wishing to engage in the sort of highly challenging work to which he has been connected for so long:

> You must be biblical in all you do and you must stay focused on Jesus. Speak simply to people, love them deeply and be there in the district for them. Unlock your area, walk into it, read the local papers and see the local problems. Do things with people, not for them. There must be no attempt simply to "get them into church". Share the task with people who burn like you. Have a taskforce in your church, if you can, who are going to be committed to the work. We have 200 raw teenage kids at our community centre. Looking after them is hard work.

You come to enjoy the ethnic mix and it's a reward to see some of the ethnic churches grow and flourish.

The church leaders, however, must live with the people – at one stage there wasn't a single Baptist pastor living within the inner ring road in London! There is such a thing as 'Redemption Lift' where people find their lives transformed by their faith, and that includes financially, so they move out of the more difficult and socially diverse areas. This can harm local churches.

I was in the Baptist ministry for 40 years and I have taken as my creed the need for three types of change: conversion to Jesus as Lord, conversion of the local church and conversion of society. I have seen whole communities that need transformed, in particular our large, run-down housing estates. We need an 'estates theology' and an 'estates ministry'. Our kind of mission has to be all about the incarnation... [7]

Loyalism, Immigration and the Christian Challenge

The multi-cultural challenge facing Bonny Downs may not be so different from the one that will face churches in Protestant working-class areas of Northern Ireland in the future. Only a few years ago, as the Troubles raged, it would have been hard to imagine Ulster as a magnet for migrants. Now, in a new era of peace and with the possible advent of a high-growth economy, as seen in the Republic of Ireland, Northern Ireland could well see some parts of its towns and cities transformed into multi-cultural spaces.

The estimated total of new arrivals in the UK in the financial year 2004/2005, based on those registering for a National Insurance Number in Northern Ireland was 12,300.[8] If Northern Ireland's economy is to grow, fresh imports of both skilled and unskilled labour will be needed and, if so, yearly immigration could rise to a multiple of that figure. In the Republic of Ireland, as the Celtic Tiger thrived, the population grew by half a million between 1996 and 2006. Admittedly a substantial number of these people were Irish 'returnees' but nonetheless the 2006 Census indicates that 10% of the Republic's population are now 'non-nationals', a figure which if it were to be transferred to the present northern context would result in a 'non-national' population of 172,000, at current demographic levels.[9]

According to the 2006 School Census for Northern Ireland, the number of children in early schooling who have a first language other than English increased from 1,800 in 2005 to 2,400 in 2006 – in other words, three out of every 200 primary-school children. Between May 2004 and March 2007, 4% of all those who registered with the Workers Registration Scheme in the UK were aiming to work in Northern Ireland although the population of the province makes up just 3% of the UK population. In other words, Northern Ireland is an increasingly popular destination for migrants and that popularity is only likely to grow as – or if – this place becomes more stable and more prosperous.[10]

The impact of an ever more visible minority ethnic population adds diversity to Ulster's hitherto somewhat predictable cultural life. However, this social trend has already given rise to increasing numbers of racially-motivated attacks on people and property which at one stage led some journalists to dub Belfast the 'race hate' capital of Europe. An increasing minority ethnic population is likely to pose the greatest perceived threat to the impoverished and marginalised in our society who may be led into thinking that 'immigrants' are 'taking their jobs' and 'their houses' away from them.

Large swathes of the Loyalist working class fall into that 'marginalised' category. Already feeling 'bested' by Nationalists, they may be reluctant to be 'bested' by foreign nationals. Most migrants who arrive in search of work and a place to stay are currently more likely to be placed in the private rented sector rather than waiting for a Housing Executive property to become available. However, where Housing Executive homes are concerned, the demographic shrinkage in Protestant working-class areas means that Housing Executive accommodation for migrants is more likely to be found in Loyalist neighbourhoods, leading to an increased risk of racial tensions in areas with an all-too-recent history of cultural under-privilege, gangsterism and deep suspicion of 'difference'.

Already, in the town of Dungannon, there have been considerable tensions between a number of 'the locals' and the Portuguese migrants who make up 10% of the population.[11] Dungannon is a predominantly Nationalist town so racial problems are certainly not confined to Loyalist areas. Nonetheless, areas such as Belfast's Donegall Pass district have also witnessed, in recent times, examples of the kind of racial tensions that can affect a small Loyalist area. Protestant residents there are very aware of the area's own demographic downturn and the visible prosperity of Chinese restaurants and shops in the vicinity. Their owners who drive expensive-looking cars and are seen to employ few non-Chinese locals have, at times, been accused of turning the 'The Pass' into Belfast's own Chinatown.

Perhaps the church in Northern Ireland will find itself stimulated and revitalised by the arrival of migrant communities. In the Republic of Ireland, new migrant populations have led to the visible growth

of many local churches. But if the new surge of cultural and religious diversity is decanted into Protestant working-class areas with their legacies of problems, many churches in these areas could find themselves caught at a three-way cultural interface: facing a new multi-ethnic challenge alongside the already pressing challenge of reconnecting with Loyalist communities, and potentially having to deal with tensions between incoming migrants and local Loyalists. Without adequate planning and resources this triple challenge may be too much for many hard-pressed churches on the 'front line' to bear.

New Thinking from Atlanta, Georgia

With these specific challenges in mind, one other case study worth drawing on is Bob Lupton's 'Urban Ministries' development in the US city of Atlanta, Georgia. Despite much affluence, many citizens live in conditions of deep poverty, experiencing high levels of crime and personal dysfunction. The greatest part of the Atlanta 'underclass' is 'non-white' and so the deprivation is amplified by a sense of racial disadvantage and a history of segregation and discrimination.

Bob Lupton responded to an inner sense of call to work with America's 'forgotten poor' while serving with the US Army in Vietnam. He then left a budding business career to work with delinquent young people. Bob and his wife sold their suburban home and, along with their two sons, moved into one of Atlanta's inner-city zones where they have lived and served as neighbours among those in need. Their life's work has been all about the rebuilding of run-down communities, where families can once again flourish and children grow into healthy adults. Through FCS Urban Ministries – a non-profit organisation which he created – he has developed a number of mixed income housing developments, founded a couple of multi-ethnic congregations, started a number of local businesses, established housing for hundreds of families and initiated a wide range of services in his community.[12]

One piece of advice he offers to churches planning community engagement in areas of need is to avoid 'non-reciprocal services and programs' and to stay away from 'old paradigms of one-way giving.'[13] In his experience, 'welfare depletes self-esteem while honourable work produces dignity… reciprocity builds mutual respect while one-way giving breeds contempt.'[14] He tells us that 'people… would far rather engage in legitimate exchange than be the object of another's pity.'[15] He then goes on to explain that:

> The magic of exchange is part of God's common grace for all those He created in His image. The work of the Kingdom involves doing justice with and for those who have been excluded from the full measures of His grace…. ours is the task of modelling the highest forms of charity that include even the most vulnerable among us as valued participants. [16]

Lupton gives as an example of malignant 'non-reciprocity' some charity work done in Georgia, in the early 1960s, in which clothes were being given out for a nominal sum from a church second-hand clothes store. Limits were carefully placed on how many clothes could be taken, no credit was allowed without a note from a local pastor and all sales and recipients were recorded and reported to the central Christian Council to foil the 'greed' of those making the rounds of church clothes closets all across the city. Lupton writes:

> Can you imagine the challenging, the tightening of rules, the manipulative ploys, the counter-moves that transpired between good church folk and those they were trying to help? Like temple police, they enacted their one-sided legislation and diligently guarded the resources of the Kingdom… something seems to go wrong when one with valued resources attempts to distribute them to others in need. A subtle, unintentional message slips through. "You have nothing of worth which I desire in return." It becomes hard to be a cheerful giver. And even harder to be a cheerful recipient. [17]

In Northern Ireland where the church is still, in many quarters, tied to its own charitable traditions and to a somewhat grandiose sense of its own moral stature and social significance such advice deserves careful consideration. How might Christian churches seek to engage people living in Loyalist housing estates and inner-city terraces in a way that is both dignified and reciprocal?

How can the lives of middle-class, professional members of Christian congregations find connection with the lives of others in working-class areas? What if 'redemption lift' has helped upwardly-mobile believers from council estates and urban terraces to join those living on leafy avenues of suburbia or country roads? What happens to those left behind? In order to counter the isolation of the less well-off from the rest of society and to enable relationships hallmarked by dignity and reciprocity, Bob Lupton suggests the radical step of 're-neighbouring'.

The context for Lupton's vision of re-neighbouring is the process that he has observed in urban

America, which is commonly called 'gentrification'. At one stage, middle-class professionals were to be found in the suburbs or in satellite towns, leaving the inner city as the place where only the poor would live – a zone where, too often, poverty, crime and addiction were rife. Now, large portions of American inner cities have become redeveloped, with disused factories and warehouses being turned into chic apartments. On formerly derelict and litter-strewn streets, numerous restaurants, boutiques, wine bars, art galleries and nightclubs have sprung up.

Lupton acknowledges the huge problems that this has created for many of the urban poor, who are now being forced to vacate their home areas due to higher rents and the impact of the redeveloper's bulldozer. Many have had to migrate to more peripheral locations in search of affordable accommodation. Yet he also sees a real opportunity for what he terms 'gentrification with justice.' This is a term for the process whereby middle-class professionals with a vibrant Christian faith come back to live in the inner city and can now bring themselves to identify with the urban poor who are adjacent to them. These new neighbours now share the same space and thus feel concerned about the same community issues. Indeed the Christian professionals can 'tithe' some of their skills in professional areas such as architecture, engineering, construction, finance, property management, law, education and the arts to their local church's community outreach programme. In this way the Christian professionals can 'connect these marketplace gifts to a Kingdom vision in the city' and learn to 're-neighbour' those who otherwise would remain as struggling strangers in their midst.[18] Lupton calls for these 'technologies of compassion' to be implemented and, in particular, for a Christian attempt to ensure that redeveloped areas retain 'mixed' housing, including affordable, good quality rented real estate for those on low incomes.[19] He suggests that the skills of re-neighbouring broken communities ought to be taught in Bible colleges, seminaries and other Christian education establishments.[20]

Lupton points out that 'if rebirth is to take place, a de-concentration of poverty and brokenness must take place'[21] and that this cannot come about without 'the presence of people of faith' who are 'the greatest resource of hope and vision within any community.'[22] He warns us that 'without the presence of strong, connected neighbour-leaders who have the best interests of the community at heart, a neglected neighbourhood becomes a desperate, dead-end place.' He suggests the need for 'gentrification with a theology to guide it'[23] and contends that with the help of this theology, the church might recognise that 'there is a vast untapped reservoir of giftedness ready to channel into the work of the Kingdom. Under the Lordship of Christ these become spiritual gifts, ideally designed for the work of Biblical justice.'[24]

A Theology of 'Re-Neighbouring' for Northern Ireland?

So how appropriate is the idea of 'gentrification with justice' to Northern Ireland? Certainly gentrification is occurring in several areas. Troubled North Belfast has seen its property prices rise at a remarkable rate as streets once considered dangerous have become desirable. Even the site of the former Crumlin Road Prison is about to become a property developer's dream, to the concern of local working-class residents who wish to see more social housing. At time of writing, a development of apartments on the Ormeau Road in the south of the city, involving the former bakery, has created a range of properties at prices beyond the reach of working-class people in the immediate neighbourhood. A similar development in the vicinity of Sandy Row has already created a social disjunction with the local working-class population. There are fears in the 'Inner City East' area that the gentrification brought about by the huge new Titanic Quarter and by the redevelopment of the former Sirocco Works will impinge unfavourably on what has always been a working-class area. Ordinary people may find themselves priced out of the prestige zones they now inhabit, much as Bob Lupton has noted it happening in the USA and as other commentators have observed it occurring in places like London's Docklands and Dublin's Financial Services District on the edge of the River Liffey.

So the opportunity does arise for motivated Christians to move into these areas not just to acquire a fine new property or 'do up' an old one but to use their skills and spiritual vision to link up with their working-class neighbours and practise a community-oriented faith. But where is this kind of re-neighbouring project being preached? As Lupton suggests, a whole new theology needs to be articulated and preached, in which the purchase of a new home in a gentrified area, adjacent to a needy working-class area, may be seen as a spiritual and ethical decision, enabling committed Christians to further the work of social healing in some of the province's most deprived parts.

However, the Loyalist working-class family does not only live in inner cities but in sprawling housing estates on the edge of the city such as Tullycarnet and Rathcoole and in numerous other council developments in towns all across Ulster, from Portadown to Carrickfergus. Because of their peripheral location and often grim reputation, these estates are unlikely to be subject to gentrification and may remain as unchanged repositories of disadvantage for many years to come. Does the principle of re-neighbouring hold relevance there?

As will be seen in the final chapter, there are a few brave believers who feel the call to step out of their comfort zones, move to a council estate and endeavour to share their faith and their gifts in a reciprocal way with 'the locals'. This is a demanding task, sometimes involving all kinds of 'culture shock'. It would be best not undertaken in isolation but with the help of fellow-Christians committed to the same vision and backed by the loving support of a strong local church that has a sensitive attitude to social issues. For most people, especially those with family commitments and other personal or workplace pressures, such risk-taking may be well beyond the horizon of possibility.

But in a place as small and interconnected as Northern Ireland, is some degree of re-neighbouring possible without having to move house? Reconnection with that council estate that stands half a mile away from the church gates can surely be achieved in a number of different ways that major on reciprocity and dignity. The final chapter takes a look at some of the local faith-based groups who are already attempting to put such a reconnection into practice.

However for a dominantly middle-class church, Lupton's notion of reciprocity will mean accepting gifts from working-class communities as well as offering gifts to them. Are there features of working-class culture that we would be willing to embrace as a gift? Or are we convinced that working-class culture is trumped and transcended by middle-class values, which are, at the end of the day, superior?

Bob Lupton urges caution 'Fixing people is a dangerous business. Fixing assumes I know what the final form should be…when I presume to fix someone I shape that person with my values, doctrine, hygiene, parenting, vocabulary, housekeeping, nutrition and a host of other things. Fixing is a licence to fashion after my image one who may be uniquely created to flower in quite a different form.'[25] Lupton also reminds all those who wish to involve themselves in ministry to the needy that 'the fundamental building blocks of the kingdom are relationships. Not programs, systems or productivity' He tells his readers that they will become immersed in 'personal involvements that disrupt schedules and drain energy.'[26]

The results of the radical call of the Saviour that we read of in the Gospels are spelt out by Lupton with clarity 'The first fruits of a new world order have come and He has revealed the values of His Kingdom: vulnerability, obedience with abandon, lavish giving, faith that defies reason, volitional downward mobility.' He assures the reader that 'full-on' community involvement, in light of these prerequisites, will not be glamorous and will often contain both joy and disappointment: 'integrity and deceit, growth and brokenness, affection and hostility are the realities of life in the field where I live and work. To deny any aspect is to miss the full measure of life.'[27]

In Northern Ireland many churches have adopted ready-made schemes for seamless church growth and unfaltering Christian development – many of them coming from the elite mega-churches of the United States. Any attempt to apply some universal 'how-to' kit for 'successful' ecclesiastical growth so that it fits the task of engagement with a local Loyalist community – complete with a mission statement and business plan – simply will not work. The task is too complex; the creativity required is too subtle and extemporary. The patience needed retards any results-oriented model of growth.

The truth is that the best community workers often learn slowly, on the job, by experimenting and adapting and persisting, assisted by a sense of collegiality with others who are on the same road. Thankfully there is an increased number of community work practitioners, both here and abroad, with whom new workers can liaise, seeking advice, sharing problems and devising ideas on how to overcome them.

So it is clear from this international survey that working-class Protestants are not the only ones who feel the heat of cultural antagonism and face the pain of living in a nation where wealth and well-being are not widely shared. Christian community work undertaken in other deprived communities around the world also provides inspiration for the present and future challenges of engagement with working-class Protestants in Northern Ireland. However, undertaking a project as radical as Bob Lupton's would surely modify the traditional Northern Irish understanding of how to 'do' church and how to practice the presence of Christ in a 'fallen' world.

[1] The interview with a Dublin community worker was conducted under conditions of anonymity, January 2008.

[2] Lynsey Hanley, Estates: An Intimate History (Granta Books, 2007) pp 17, 163.

[3] The Times, 31 December 2007.

[4] For statistics regarding Newham see www.newham.gov.uk/Services/factsandfiguresaboutnewham.htm. Accessed 21 May 2007. The figure for faith-based organisations was provided by Colin Marchant, retired pastor of Bonny Downs Church in the Newham area, interviewed in London, April 2007.

[5] See http://www.transformnewham.com/Group/Group.aspx?id=50158. Accessed 4 July 2007.

[6] Information on all aspects of the Bonny Downs work can be found at www.bonnydownschurch.org/bonnydowns/index/html; www.bonnydowns.org/BDCA/flandersfield.html; www.bonnydowns.org/BDCA/thewell.html;www.bonnydowns.org/BDCA/index.html. Accessed 4 August 2007.

[7] Interview with Colin Marchant, London, 12 April 2007.

[8] For this information see the section devoted to demography on www.nisra.gov.uk/demography/default.asp3.htm. Accessed 18 August 2007.

[9] See www.cso.ie/census/Census2006_Principal_Demographic_Results.htm. Accessed 19 August 2007.

[10] See www.nisra.gov.uk/demography/default.asp3.htm. Accessed 20 August 2007.

[11] *The Irish News*, 16 June 2004.

[12] Robert D Lupton, *Renewing the City: Reflections on Community Development and Urban Renewal* (Inter Varsity Press, 2005), pp 239-240.

[13] Robert D Lupton, *Compassion, Justice and the Christian Life: Rethinking Ministry to the Poor* (Regal Books, 2007), p 10.

[14] Ibid, p 27.

[15] Ibid, p 42.

[16] Ibid, p 44.

[17] From an article entitled 'Clothes Closets and Compassion' from *Urban Perspectives... reflections on faith, grace and the city* (March 2007) on http://www.fcsministries.org/up/index.html. Accessed 20 July 2007.

[18] Robert D Lupton, *Compassion, Justice and the Christian Life: Rethinking Ministry to the Poor* (Regal Books, 2007), p 9.

[19] Ibid., p 10.

[20] Ibid., p 16.

[21] Ibid., p 99.

[22] Ibid., p 108.

[23] Ibid., p 116.

[24] Ibid., p 117.

[25] Robert D Lupton, *Theirs is the Kingdom: Celebrating the Gospel in Urban America* (Harper Collins, 1989), p 46.

[26] Ibid., p 75.

[27] Ibid., pp 105-113.

6

a record of engagement

The final chapter is given over to some recent and ongoing practitioners of Christian involvement with Protestant, mostly working-class communities and also the churches or projects where they have been based. What follows is the product of a series of interviews, mainly conducted during the autumn of 2007. It is not meant to be an example of best practice, but rather to offer a sample of what is happening where Christian men and women clearly feel the 'call' both to connect with raw human need and to create a fresh profile for the church of Jesus Christ.

Christian community involvement is rarely a solo effort. Most of the interviewees were engaged as part of a team, whether large or small. Individuals from outside a working-class context who make a solitary attempt to connect, may well find themselves alienated and disappointed. One particular friend of the author, motivated by a broadly spiritual and moral quest for connection, recently purchased a house in a Loyalist housing estate and attempted to live there. The effort was clearly a courageous one and an intense 'learning curve' but it was an experience characterised by cultural disorientation, fraught with fear of the looming paramilitary presence, devoid of a path for creating personal relationships with his neighbours and soon abandoned.[1]

There are, of course, people out there in the statutory and voluntary sector doing selfless and positive things for other people without explicitly Christian motives. While social compassion may be the product of a Christian faith, it is certainly not confined to Christians and may be found in places that Evangelical believers are surprised to see it. The words of one community worker in a Loyalist estate in County Antrim should bear this out. This particular person is employed in a mediation centre that was established by a paramilitary unit which has recently been attempting to resolve social problems by exclusively peaceful means.

'It's very often us who will be there for the people, dealing with disputes over property and wills, marriage difficulties, anti-social behaviour and so on. We are there if needed when there are 50 kids standing around on a Saturday night, drinking Buckfast. The phone is lifted to us all the time. I have had requests of help from people whose children have just attempted to commit suicide. I have accompanied people to the hospital on several occasions. We get the respect. We are there to help because we care for our communities....'

Pastor Joe White, Downpatrick Baptist Church, County Down

As has already been shown, Christian engagement with social need is not a new thing. The small Protestant council estate centred on Bridge Street, in the largely Nationalist town of Downpatrick, is instructive in this regard. Currently, a small Baptist community worships adjacent to this estate and as Pastor Joe White points out, they attempt to reach out to the people:

We have a very successful Sunday lunch every month, after the church service. Caring and sharing you might call it. We open the church doors and spill outside into Bridge Street when we eat our lunches, so we can talk to local people. Once, recently... the whole day's worship and fellowship went on from 10.45am to 4.45pm! Our relationship with Bridge Street is very important as it is the only Protestant enclave in the town and has its fair share of problems. But the church's mission is to care for the broken and the mixed up. We have recently bought and refurbished a nearby hall, which had been built in the 19th century. Now we use it for social events and for outreach, especially through our youth worker.

The Baptists of the 21st century are continuing work undertaken in the 1990s by a local independent 'community church', under the leadership of local businessman, John Thompson, which had purchased extensive premises close to Bridge Street and made innovative attempts to help the young people of the neighbourhood. However both modern churches stand in an Evangelical tradition that goes back to the 19th century, when another local Christian businessman called Pilson, who was engaged with charitable work in the town, established a hall which provided a warm welcome to local working-class people who could meet there for religious services in an informal environment less intimidating than that of a traditional church building. This is the very hall that the Baptists have purchased in recent times.

Rev Noel Agnew, West Kirk Presbyterian Church, Shankill Road, Belfast

Frequently, it is the minister who carries the biggest load of responsibility for initiating and sustaining an individual church's response to a local working-class community. The Presbyterian minister, Noel Agnew came from Scotland to Northern Ireland some years ago and leads the congregation of West Kirk church in the west of the city, in the intensely Loyalist Shankill district which shows all the signs of social and economic change as heavy industry has closed and the population of the area has shrunk, partly in response to the vicious paramilitary feuds of recent years. There are signs that its proximity to the city centre in a time of greater peace may actually make the Shankill area a much more desirable place to live even though some Presbyterian congregations in this part of the city have already contemplated closing their doors due to falling rolls.

A mentality often exists today in which the church and the ordinary people are scared of one another. The church in some places has retreated inside its fortress and pulled up the drawbridge and never gone out again since. I have tried to get the church at West Kirk to open up to the Shankill Road on which it stands. I hope that locals now say, 'That is the church that opens its doors….'

Amongst our weekly activities we now have a very successful men's breakfast. Over thirty men come along. There are some fellows with a difficult background. The local branch of Alcoholics Anonymous also meets in church on a Wednesday night. We also have taken over a nearby community centre in Conway Street where local people can come along and share their lives with us. The man in charge is actually a Free Presbyterian and a former UDA member. He knows people well, understands them and talks their language.

On the night I was installed, one of the speakers said to the congregation 'Free this man up to work the road.' That's what I do. I can walk along the Shankill and I have six conversations before I return. I regularly visit two pubs on the Shankill – the Royal Bar and the Berlin Arms. No, of course I don't wear my collar when I go in there. I hardly ever wear it on the road. If I do, people say to me 'Who's dead?' When I am in the pubs, I do not drink alcohol. It is all about making contact with people whom I would regard as my friends. Frequently I just end up listening. I may never see the full benefit of what I am doing but at least I hope that by showing this kind of friendship I am giving the gospel some credibility. Too many church people just scuttle in and out of the inner city in their cars.

I would like to see closer bonds between the churches, especially the amalgamation of the ones in my own denomination. We are too splintered. There has been inter-denominational outreach in the past but there is still really too much of an 'our building' approach. Unfortunately those outside the churches don't feel so fondly about those church buildings. One young man said to me about West Kirk, 'Noel, that big building is off-putting.'

I would like to see Christian people moving into the Shankill to live rather than moving out. It was such a proud community sixty years ago when the shipyard employed people on these streets. You were either a shipyard man or a man who worked in Mackies' factory and you held your head high as you walked down the road. Now there are plenty of men who spend their entire day in the pub. Some drink themselves into oblivion. Our job is to try to reach out to men like that.

Rev Canon Trevor Williams, Holy Trinity and St Silas with Immanuel, North Belfast

In few places has the ministerial burden been more fraught with difficulty than in North Belfast, which contains a patchwork of rival communities and tense interfaces. It is particularly difficult for ministers whose parishes included the people involved in the infamous Holy Cross Primary School dispute of 2001/2002, between the Protestant and Catholic communities of Upper Ardoyne. Trevor Williams, the Church of Ireland rector of Holy Trinity and St Silas with Immanuel is attempting to establish valuable partnerships with key players of every allegiance in the community life of North Belfast. He is also trying to expand on the possible community roles that his church might play and to build good relations with local people in all kinds of practical ways.

> The 'Holy Cross' dispute took place just outside our doors and there was a lot of alienation from the church because we felt we could not support the stand that many in the local community were taking. That has been largely repaired, thankfully. We have now taken part in the local Community Empowerment Project and we have also endeavoured to implement Tearfund's 'Church, Community and Change' scheme which helps congregations to reach out to their neighbourhoods. One Saturday every month we have about a hundred local residents in to our community breakfast, which is a good Ulster Fry. It's a very useful connecting point between the church and the local people. With support from Tearfund and the Church of Ireland Priorities Fund we have employed a part time Family Support Worker focussed on families who do not access support services.
>
> We have worked with other groups including the Ballysillan Upper Ardoyne Neighbourhood Partnership. We are hoping to receive funding to build a doctor's surgery and pharmacy on the church grounds. We have also put in a bid to receive a grant to develop our church hall as a 'Healthy Living Centre', devoted to offering the community all kinds of therapeutic and beneficial facilities. We would see ourselves as also working as closely as possible with other churches in North Belfast, including the local Catholic congregations. I myself meet with a number of other clergy on a monthly basis.

Rev Tom Wilson, Kilmakee Presbyterian Church, Dunmurry

Rev Tom Wilson is the minister of Kilmakee Presbyterian Church in Dunmurry. This too is a Loyalist working-class context but a rather different one to North Belfast. Several decades ago this was a village on the outskirts of Belfast but has now become swallowed up in the city's westward sprawl. The church is adjacent to the Seymour Hill estate, which has a stable population and a good reputation as a pleasant place to live in the district – defying the notion that all Protestant working-class environments are grim. Tom's ministry has included a lot of involvement in the civic life of this estate but has also included a more significant amount of cross-community activity than might have been considered possible in such a Loyalist context.

> Kilmakee church is situated in the Seymour Hill Estate and has 200 committed members. The church building has been here now for going on fifty years. Recently we have been offered a £28,000 grant by the Community Relations Council to install a bank of computers so that we can further the cross-community work that we have been doing, particularly in regard to the links between our young people and a Catholic group centred at St Louis House in Andersonstown. However a few years ago we felt the need to build more connections with our Protestant working-class base in Seymour Hill. So we applied for some Community Relations Council money in order to carry out a 'community audit' in order to see what the needs and the strengths of the estate actually were.
>
> On the basis of the audit, help became available to Seymour Hill from the Community Convention, which had been set up to help Protestant, Loyalist and Unionist communities boost their 'social capital'. This meant bringing key players in the local community together such as schools, churches and residents' associations. We addressed such issues as housing. We have an imbalance here, to do with the fact that there is a list of families waiting to find a home in the estate and yet there are family-sized homes in Seymour Hill now occupied by a single older person who is the last person in their family residing there.
>
> We also tried to tackle the issue of paramilitary murals, so as to make the atmosphere less threatening. However a really big topic for consideration was education. One of our fears was that the local Dunmurry High School would be closed down due to falling numbers although that situation now seems to have been reversed. We also wanted to maintain our local primary school, as provision of on-site early education is deemed essential for the continued well-being and viability of the estate. I suppose that we would really like to see good community schooling for our children so that they could be educated on the same campus throughout their years in education. One other task which we at Kilmakee involved ourselves in, together with the other groups already mentioned, was the drawing up of a community charter for the neighbourhood, which highlights the rights and responsibilities of the local people and informs the readers of local facilities and amenities.
>
> A reasonably high proportion of our church members are residents of Seymour Hill. I would

say that this estate offers quite a good quality of life. There is relatively little crime and the housing is well laid-out and well maintained. It is demographically stable and a lot of families have been here since the estate was created, half a century ago. It is also well located for access to both Belfast and Lisburn. The UDA has been the influential paramilitary organisation but it does not seem to have been behaving aggressively in the community. However flags and bonfires are very prevalent in the summer months. We have had occasional unpleasant incidents such as when a car belonging to someone attending our church, which had a southern registration, was deliberately scratched. I guess it is true that if space is found to erect new homes in the area, then the families moving in will be more Protestant ones.

There are several challenges involved in trying to place the local church at the heart of community development as we have tried to do. Some people think that you should confine yourself to 'preaching the gospel' and that community involvement is a 'waste of time'. Then there is the issue as to whether you will lose your power and independence when you are part of an 'umbrella' group. Above all, there is the matter of time and energy being sapped. It is a danger for me as a minister but also for the people in the small core group that forms the heart of any church. This is especially the case when you are trying desperately to 'get up to the pace' in understanding how to access funding and how both the statutory and the voluntary sector work. You can spend two days trying to collect the information to fill in a grant application form. I simply couldn't do all this by myself and a number of key individuals with the right kind of experience have made all the difference in progressing our community work. Sometimes I have actually had to tell them to stop doing something that is too much of a burden to expect them to carry.

In terms of defining an ethos for what we try to do, you could take as an influential example the 'servant evangelism' of the Vineyard Church. We seek to let the estate know that we are here to help. For instance, our young people worked on cleaning up the area during the holidays. We try to do separate nights for our own youth in the church and for outreach to youngsters from outside the congregation who live in Seymour Hill. However many of our own young people are from the estate and they readily involve themselves in the worship. Our older teens are doing useful work on issues of faith and identity prior to meeting with their Catholic counterparts.

The church group and the outreach group have different needs and exhibit different kinds of behaviour. Some of the young lads from Seymour Hill are difficult although they can start to mellow. Occasionally we have had damage done to the premises overnight but we now feel safe about reporting those responsible to the residents' association, with whom we have a good relationship, and we know that they will not now be subject to brutal punishment-beatings. This year my wife and I took a bunch of rather troublesome lads to our house in Portstewart for a few days. We took them out to church on Sunday, where they proceeded to sit in the front rows and, after talking for a bit, some of them fell asleep during the sermon!

Elma and Karen, Ballynahinch Baptist Church, Co Down

Although men are by far the most likely to be at the head in Northern Ireland's churches, it is clear that women often play an important role in community development work, very often focusing on the needs of other women. Elma and Karen from the Baptist church in Ballynahinch, County Down provide evidence of this kind of work. Their interview also offers a view of a Christian community that is unashamedly evangelistic in ethos, yet deeply committed to a social gospel, in which local believers recognise that they must be prepared to work in partnership with others, to generate a more vibrant and equitable civic life. The church's outreach to the nearby Loyalist council estate is only one part of a diverse engagement with the entire town in which it is situated – a town whose demographic profile also includes a sizeable Catholic population and a considerable number of comfortably middle-class inhabitants.

Our vision statement in the church reads: 'To see the making and maturing of fully committed disciples of Jesus Christ, to the glory of God.' How do we achieve this aim? By pursuing what we call the Ballynahinch 'Bs' – Bridge, Belong, Build, Body and Beacon. Part of that vision for our church is to reach out to the whole community. Our church is on the doorstep of Langley Road, a strongly Loyalist estate where we have been concentrating a lot of our effort. Two years ago, we partnered with the Langley residents' group to secure a community house that could be used to build relationships and hold events of interest to the locals. In particular we have worked with a group of women whom we have now got to know really well. Although many of these women don't normally attend church, we believe that God is at work in their lives. We have developed a

friendship and an openness to talk about the problems they may be experiencing.

Some of the things we have created so far are beauty evenings, photography clubs, cookery classes and flower arranging sessions. Some of these have been funded by East Down Rural Community Network. We have also gone for a day's outing to Dublin. We meet each Thursday morning for coffee and the chat can be about anything. It is amazing how often and how naturally the conversation gets around to spiritual things. Some of the girls have joined our discipleship group and come along to church. This developing friendship is real and is not dependent on those who are involved embracing the Christian gospel, even though we long for them to do so.

Befriending these twenty or so girls has meant getting alongside them in all kinds of ways. For instance when one or two of them have had to go to hospital, we have gone along with them and offered to pray for them when they are unwell. One of the girls who had been an alcoholic for 10 years has stopped drinking for a year now and although she has not become a Christian, she believes that she has been empowered to stop the alcohol because of prayer. We also had a Christmas dinner with the group and we try to find other occasions to celebrate together. We are hoping to host a Valentine's Day meal in the church, providing an opportunity for the girls to bring their partners.

We have also tried to help with parenting issues and just recently tackled the issue of drug awareness. We are also involved with the Besom project within the church, which provides items of furniture and practical help from our members for those in need in the community. The need is sourced through social workers and through various agencies and has been particularly taken up by single-parent families. We have tried to be real with the girls. We have tried all kinds of things to build relationships with them. They have been to our homes for supper and we have been invited to some of their homes. Recently we did a course on the issues of identity and self-worth, entitled 'Through the Looking Glass' and hope to provide other courses, tackling specific issues such as anger.

We try to reach out to more than just a few women. We have gone around the doors in Ballynahinch, giving out copies of the *Challenge* magazine, which contains both secular and Christian articles. Once a year we invite the local community in for a neighbourhood supper. We have worked alongside local people, doing litter-lifts. We have tried to reach the men in our community with several of our themed creative services, including a motorbike evening called 'Rev It Up' when we made contact with the local motorbike club and had bikes and bike memorabilia in the church. Next time we do a bikers' service we would like to do a barbeque as well. We are convinced that there is a very real appetite for and interest in spiritual things; it is all a matter of putting things across in a way that makes sense to the community around us. 'This is so different from the church we knew as kids' one of the girls said recently, after one of our church services.

At Easter our church members brought in lots of small Easter eggs and we went door-to-door, giving them out. At Christmas time we conducted a similar exercise with packets of fudge. Again this highlights the presence of our church in the community and gives us an opportunity to bless people and to show God's love and personal interest. Because of the Besom project we have had the chance to partner with social workers to help those in need. We have sent a team out to paint peoples' houses in the wider community. We would like to help in situations where people are dealing with debt problems. A couple of us are planning to attend a conference in the near future, where we can learn more about counselling those who are struggling with debt and the difficulties of managing on a meagre income.

We have been fortunate in our relationship with the paramilitaries on the Langley Road who at first were annoyed at the thought of us 'coming into' their estate and 'taking over' their community house but they have come to recognise that we are there as guests to help the community in any way we can.

Undoubtedly in our church there is a lot of talent and creativity and we have been fortunate to have leadership who give us the freedom for these gifts to be used. Our Creative Services provide opportunities to invite the community along to church. These services are held every six to eight weeks and are designed around a contemporary theme. We held an evening service recently on the theme of 'Narnia' and had an Easter service called 'The Day God Died'. On this occasion, one of our team made a huge cross, which was then brought into the church and held up for everyone to see as the pastor did his talk. An opportunity was given for everyone to come up and dip their hand into red paint and make a palm print on the cross to show our involvement in the crucifixion. On another occasion we had a sports event on the theme of rugby, entitled 'Try Conversion'. Huge rugby posts were put up as a background and we invited the Irish rugby star Andrew Trimble to come along and talk to us about being a Christian and a professional sportsman. Last Valentine's Day, we again held a special creative event entitled 'It must be Love'. Afterwards one of the girls, when hearing our pastor speak about God's love became very emotional and said 'I don't believe in God, but there is certainly something in this.' A Community Sunday is held twice a year, when we invite various representatives from our community to do a talk about their work e.g. a policeman, teacher, or the local suicide prevention officer, who does a very important job, considering that the town has high suicide rate. This service gives us the opportunity to pray for them, show our appreciation and see if there is any way we can help.

Every Friday night a team from some of the local churches goes onto the streets and offers coffee to young people while another team stays behind and prays. Our church is in the process of building enlarged premises and once this has been completed we hope to use it in different ways to be a witness to our local community.

We are always on the lookout for new ideas to capture the significance of current events and through them project the wonderful good news of the Christian gospel. It is important that church leadership is wholly supportive. A recent service focused on leaders as servants and looked at the story of Jesus washing the disciples' feet. In order to show the reality of this, several of our church leaders got down and washed the feet of members of the congregation. Not a new idea perhaps but just as out of line with contemporary concepts of leadership as it was in Jesus' day.

We will keep trying.

Lynn Duff, Senior Youth Pastor, Carrickfergus Community Church, County Antrim

Lynn Duff is a youth pastor connected to the Community Church and Café, situated on the Sunnylands Estate in Carrickfergus, County Antrim. Not only does Lynn's interview give evidence of a high level of commitment to the welfare of the community it also shows a real desire on the part of her Christian colleagues to 'do church' on terms that will not alienate a working-class community. At the time of the interview, Carrickfergus Loyalism was appearing in the media for all the wrong reasons, due to an ongoing feud between factions in the UDA, which resulted in injury to a number of civilians and a police officer.

We started the café in Sunnylands in 1997 although the group of Christians behind the project began meeting in the estate back in 1992. Since then we have built an extension to the cafe where our church meets. We are now constructing an entirely new church building on a nearby site. We originally bought our land from the council and then we had to get the money to do the building, using a mix of grants, donations and funds that the members raised themselves by doing such things as remortgaging their houses.

The café soon became our meeting point with the community. We serve meals at cost price and pensioners can eat for free on Tuesdays though they usually leave a donation. There are lots of people who use the café who haven't become Christians or a part of the church but who look to the pastor to help them at key moments in life. He has dedicated the children of several couples, married couples and he has buried old folk who have no other links with religious organisations. Both the clientele in the café and the membership of the church are mostly made up of working-class people and that includes a lot of singles and divorcees. There would be few 'complete' families.

I am the youth pastor and currently I mentor two girls in our church who, among other things, go out and visit senior citizens in their homes. We have an 'Over-60s club' which meets twice a month. At the other end of the scale, the girls are volunteering with a local primary school. I also do a lot of work with local schools. I go in and help take Scripture Union meetings. I teach Personal and Social Development at Carrickfergus College and Carrickfergus Grammar, focusing on building up the young peoples' self-esteem. I also take a girls' group here in the church. A boys' group is beginning, led by some of our own young men, who are undergoing training as youth workers.

An estate like Sunnylands can be a dark place, in need of light. What I mean is that there is a great deal of hopelessness and there is a feeling that life has always been like this and it won't change. It's not that there isn't money about or that people are homeless. It's just that so many of them live a poor life in other ways, dependent on benefits and seeing no other way to exist. There is much bad health. Children are not encouraged by their parents to achieve, they are left to run around the streets at all hours and they are often sent out to school with sweets and crisps for lunch. Many youngsters are the offspring of teenage parents who themselves were not particularly cared for when they were growing up. Often there is a resentment of those who have 'moved up' and 'got out'.

However, as an expression of our identification with the community, several of us have now acquired houses in the estate. Some of us work in part-time jobs that enable us to give volunteer energy to the church community. You have to remember that Jesus lived his life in the community and was there for needy people. The church didn't tolerate poverty in the early days either, helping one another as they saw fit. A number of us also try to go downtown at the weekends and keep an eye on things, particularly when the pubs shut. We go around the town centre at night, praying for God's presence on the streets and making sure that some of the young people who have got drunk can find a safe way home. We get prayer requests from people who are worried about something and who will talk about it openly when they have had too much to drink. There have been suicides recently in the town and we pray about that. We have also intervened at times to try to prevent fights breaking out. Usually we stay out from 11.00pm till 1.00am.

The community police used to be more present in Sunnylands. They are sporadic now. Perhaps they are overstretched. Many of the kids just call them 'the filth' now and run away when they see them coming whereas there used to be a bit of familiar banter between the police officers and the young people. However, we will work with the police in any way we can. And we will work with any of the statutory bodies in the attempt to help Sunnylands. They are the professionals, not us. It's important to work together with the estate's community centre and the tenants' association. We partner with them, creating fun activities for the community, coming up to 'The Twelfth'.

It's crucial not to duplicate work that others are doing. This applies to our relationship with other churches in the area. So our young people have joined forces with the local Baptist Youth Group to do a single joint summer scheme. That way we actually get more done than if we had been working separately and appearing as rivals. We may not see eye to eye on all theological matters and we may worship in rather different ways but the differences don't emerge when you are working hard together. But we don't just focus on the needs of Sunnylands in our church. We have tried to think about the global community. We tell our members that 'small' people can make a difference. We explain that for the price of two Chinese meals per month they can sponsor a child in Africa.

How did we end up in Sunnylands rather than somewhere else? My father, who is the pastor, once owned a business on the Crumlin Road in Belfast and he sold it, gave his money away and started Christian work. My parents moved in 1987 to a place called 'The Haven' in Templepatrick where they pastored a Christian community and farm where people were enabled to 'get off' drugs, break with paramilitarism and make a fresh start. Then they heard that there was a desire in Carrickfergus for a community church. They began to meet to pray in different peoples' homes and then in community centres in several estates. Eventually they decided on Sunnylands as a suitable place on which to focus. And so the work began.

As a church we believe strongly in spiritual healing. We have a 'prayer clinic' that started off as a place for local people to bring their physical ailments to God in order to be healed but we soon discovered that inner healings were just as sought after. People were bringing terrible things such as abuse to the clinic for prayer. And we also believe in the importance of leadership. Not heavy 'shepherding', just good, sensible leadership. So many of the people we know do not have a united family and a parent who can guide them. They need someone to be there for them, to advise them and to motivate them.

Linda Armitage, former Director of Youth and Community Work, East Belfast Mission, Lower Newtownards Road, Belfast

Linda Armitage worked at East Belfast Mission for several years and has subsequently moved on to another post. This mission is run by the Methodist Church and there are ambitious plans afoot to develop an 'urban village' on site, with a Christian ethos, to be known as the Skainos Project. Much of Linda's work was with Loyalist working-class women in the vicinity of the Lower Newtownards Road, among whom she found a real willingness to engage in self-development, although the process was often a slow one. This is an area of the inner city whose inhabitants have felt the full force of post-industrial decline. Now there are new challenges. Development projects in the new, vaunted 'Titanic Quarter' and on the site of the old Sirocco Works will surely change the character of the area in a way that may not be congenial to working-class people. Hopefully, the Skainos Project will do much to address this issue.

When I arrived at the East Belfast Mission, about seven years ago, there had been a mother and toddler group in existence for quite some time. However I noticed that there were very few women and children who came from the working-class streets around the mission. Also, the group itself lacked structure and purpose – the mums just sat around drinking tea while the children created a lot of noise together. I talked to the leaders and they agreed with me that a program was needed so we decided to plan activities that included craft, art and music. I also talked to the local health centre and to the local 'Surestart' group, which specialises in offering educational help to pre-school children and their mothers. They swiftly offered their support. Soon we had a number of local girls and their children well involved. In due course we were able to train up some of them to be their own project leaders.

It was out of the mother and toddler project that a separate women's group emerged. Some of them were saying 'Why don't we meet without the kids?' and so by 2005 a group was formed. At first, I provided the leadership but gradually I went to less and less of the meetings. This was deliberate, as I wanted to enable them to take charge of their own development. The agreed aim was to offer personal development through the arts and also to promote the practice of help and support for one another. We managed to get a very good facilitator – a highly creative and spiritual man – who chairs the fortnightly meetings and does a wide range of things with the women. Of course much more goes besides the regular meetings. Individuals need help at moments of crisis such as spells in hospital. We also organise special outings and trips.

This women's group is intergenerational. Their ages range from 17 to 60 and we regard that as a strength because they can all learn from one another. They are very happy coming into the mission to meet, even though our buildings are scarcely all that attractive or modern. They know that we won't try to evangelise them in the traditional sense though there is hardly a meeting goes by in which God is not talked about in some context or other. The women raise the topic themselves. Occasionally someone will ask 'So are you'se not going to try to convert us yet?' I also find that I get lots of questions about how I do my parenting, such as 'Do you mean to say you don't put TVs in the kids' bedrooms?' A number of the women are now sending their children along to youth activities at the mission, such as the Dance Nation group, which is composed of young local girls.

Do some of the women come to faith and join in the church services? Yes, some do. And some others are on the fringe of the church, engaging with core church members at activities like the bowls night. Others do not commit to church life in any way. It's not that they feel 'anti-God'. It's just that many of them think they are not 'good enough' and some feel that they would have to give up the things that Ulster Evangelicalism has always prohibited such as booze and fags.

In truth we believe that many people have to 'belong' before they start to 'believe', which is the opposite of what some Evangelical churches practice. In any case we will allow people to 'belong' to our mission even if they never show signs of faith. In that regard I can think of one wee old alcoholic man who came in to our café every day for a meal to 'line his stomach' before he started into a day's drinking. He never came to the church. But when he was ill, some of our staff took him round a meal. And when he died a lot of the folk from the mission were the ones who attended his funeral.

Our approach to youth work would also be a careful, relational one. We try to be pastoral and positive with the children and do things with them that will build their ability to cope with life. It's not exactly the traditional Ulster 'children's meeting'. We have a number of volunteers who help with our youth work and although the amount of time they give is always going to be limited, the fact that they are involved is great because many of them are either working class, like the kids themselves or else from a working-class background. No, these people haven't been separated from their roots by 'redemption lift' and definitely do want to contribute to the East Belfast community.

During the fortnightly women's group meetings, they have done a whole host of things, all geared towards building confidence, enabling communication and promoting participation. The artistic activities have ranged from jewellery-making to dance. They did a longer project called 'St Patrick, Prods and Prams.' This took them deeper into issues of culture and identity. They learnt to grasp the difference between myth and truth and they ended up actually taking part in the St Patrick's Day Festival in the city centre although they were scared stiff about doing so. Some of their men-folk said 'You can't do that – it's a Catholic thing.' However the girls explained that that was a myth and that no, it didn't have to be a 'Catholic thing'. They had really learnt something in the process of the course.

The next project they did was about faith and values and that went even deeper into key issues. One of the topics that came up for discussion was racism. This is important, as there are now a number of women from other ethnic backgrounds and faiths coming along to our toddler group. It takes time working on attitudes and we have slowly got the women to question some of their beliefs about ethnic minorities. Hopefully they can then pass this on to their children. We now actually have an Asian lady as one of the leaders in the toddlers' group and that would not have been possible at the beginning.

However, it is important not to impose a set of middle-class values on these women. There are certain things about working-class life that are very positive. People in these streets don't worry so much about long-term issues or make long-term plans and very often they spend as they earn. At its best it is all about living life to the full in the present moment! Having said that, it's possibly more difficult for a parent to pass down positive values to their children in a working-class context. There are so many other influences out there on the working-class street where the kids spend so much of their time. One thing that must be mentioned is the absence of working-class males in our work. The truth is that a lot of the women we work with do not have men in their lives at all and are raising their children alone. Others have men at home but those men spend much of the evening in the pub and offer little companionship. We need more males to initiate some kind of work with these men but I am afraid that 80% of all community workers are women.

How did I get involved with this kind of work? I guess it starts with how I was brought up. I saw Jesus in the attitudes of my mother. Our home was 'always open' and you never knew who you might have found sharing a meal with you around the dinner table. When I became a Christian I very soon saw Jesus as a radical who was prepared to get totally involved in peoples' lives. I went to Bible College in Bournemouth in England, which freed me greatly and opened my eyes to social justice issues on the streets of that town. I worked with homeless people. I worked with gays. I lived next door to a brothel. In later years I went to Bob Lupton's mission in Atlanta, Georgia and did six months training there within the inner city context where I witnessed and experienced segregation, racism and prejudice at first hand and learnt a great deal that would stand me in good stead when I returned home.

Now I am leaving my work at East Belfast Mission. The seven years have been great but most of the groups I helped get started have become self-led and, as I have done what I can, it's now time for me to move on. All Christian work is for a season. I would say to all Christians who want to be involved in this kind of community outreach that it is very, very hard work. You have to stay in tune with God. That is vital. And do your work naturally but don't be afraid of talking about Jesus. Remember that work like this takes time. It happens in God's season, not yours.

The Vine Centre, Crumlin Road, Belfast

Although much of the interaction between concerned Christians and needy communities is focused on the work of the local church, there has been a growth in recent years of Christian community organisations which operate as separate entities – although they may have a close relationship with a particular church or denomination. These centres often make innovative efforts, born out of biblical convictions, to practise intensive social involvement with troubled Protestant areas of Northern Ireland. One such organisation is The Vine Centre, situated on Belfast's Crumlin Road. The centre currently employs 23 employees and 20 volunteers. It is also a useful venue for students who are training at institutions such as Belfast Bible College to gain an insight into faith-based community work.

This project, the seeds of which were sown during the early years of the Troubles, has expanded greatly in recent years and occupies a spacious new building on an arterial route that forms the boundary between the West and North of the city and is very much lacking in the commercial and social vibrancy that still characterises the nearby Shankill Road, despite years of overall community decline. Funding comes from a number of sources in the statutory and voluntary sector. A wide range of activities is offered at The Vine to the working-class Protestant community that surrounds it. There are facilities for Arts and Crafts and there is a range of computer training available, through classes delivered by the nearby Belfast Metropolitan College. Training is also offered in the basic skills needed for labourers who wish to gain certification for work on building sites.

There is also a range of after-school activities available for local children. There have been classes that provide tuition for the Eleven Plus exam, in an area of the city where educational aspiration and attainment have been very limited. Adults can also benefit from advice sessions given in areas of concern such as housing and benefits. Other assistance provided down through the years at the centre has included help offered to young females by a Pregnancy Advice Service and a series of group sessions in the crucial area of Suicide Prevention. More individually focused pastoral help and counselling may also be offered from a Christian perspective.

Youth work continues to be a staple feature of The Vine and one of the key challenges in this area has been the animosity between children who have been caught on either side in the bitter UDA/UVF feuds. Another characteristic of the centre has been its role as a 'neutral' venue for mediation work within the Protestant community and between that community and nearby Nationalists. The Vine tries hard to connect to local churches, many of whom are struggling with the impact of demographic change but are happy, if they can, to provide volunteer assistance at the centre. Certainly the venue itself gives a strong sense of being somewhere that celebrates its host community. High-quality photos of local people and institutions hang on every available wall and the rooms are mostly named after local people who have contributed to the well-being of the local people or have excelled in some way.

The Bridge Community Association, Lower Ravenhill Road, East Belfast

Another centre which has contributed greatly to the well-being of its host community is The Bridge, based in the Lower Ravenhill area. It was initiated as a response to the results of survey work carried out in the area – cited earlier in this publication – which showed a weak relationship between local churches and the local people. The account that follows is the result of an interview with a particular person who once worked at The Bridge and who reflects on the challenges, the problems and also the deep strengths and rewards of this kind of community involvement.

> The Bridge was really founded in the 1980s out of a sense that working-class areas were alienated from the Christian church. Maurice Kinkead, when working as a Baptist College student in Finaghy, became very aware that going to working-class peoples' doors and offering them invitations to come to church was simply not working as a strategy. He talked with like-minded people inside the denomination and then they got together and looked for a place to start some serious Christian outreach that would establish genuine relationships between Christians and the urban working-class world of which it knew so little.
>
> The Bridge, as it was to be called, began by renovating a property in the Ravenhill area and turning it into an advice centre and a café for the community. Gradually The Bridge moved away from its purely Baptist roots although it has tried to retain as much as possible of its Christian

ethos. You might say that the centre received some criticism from those Evangelicals who, after a while, could see that the venture was not producing 'results' in terms of 'conversions'. Well, you could reply that neither was the traditional form of gospel mission producing large numbers of 'conversions' either. Anyway, we were in there for the long term and we would want to measure the success of the centre in wider terms than 'the number of souls saved.'

My frustration is that Northern Irish Evangelical churches are happy to see outreach involving healthcare, education and housing in foreign missions, many miles from home. Yet they don't want to make the connection to practical mission here at home. The gospel here had long ago become identified in Protestant working-class communities with a certain kind of 'good-living' lifestyle. No smoking, no drinking and no going to dances. We at The Bridge deliberately tried to go beyond that image to a more positive and biblical one, which has to do with being converted in order to start loving your neighbour. As Maurice Kinkead once said to me 'We are here to confuse people as to what Christianity is all about'. But sadly the damage had often already been done. I was aware of a Women's Group at The Bridge who had all 'got saved' at an early age but not one of whom now went anywhere near a church. They all now felt that a Christian commitment as a young person did not mean anything. It's hard to try and show people like that a better vision of a Christian commitment. It's harder for them to unlearn something than to learn it.

We soon saw it as our task to broaden out the centre by creating a 'Bridge Community Association' which was Christian in its commitment but which now involved a partnership with several local churches and above all with the local people, many of whom by now were users of the centre. You have to work with people and not just for them. Anyway, because we were now recipients of quite a number of charitable grants and government monies, which were being dedicated to the welfare of our part of the city, we felt that it was not suitable for The Bridge's original board to be the only ones dictating how it would be spent. We had to share power. By working alongside non-Christians in the running of the Bridge's many affairs, we would be creating the opportunity for those people to share our lives and witness at close quarters what a living faith is all about.

Many of the local people in the area undoubtedly were and are deprived, even though there are more jobs and there is more wealth in working-class homes than in the 1980s. Deprivation is all about lack of opportunity and many people in the area experience that. They may have a colour TV in the house but no colouring pencils for the children to draw with. Education doesn't enter their minds as a road to a better and happier life. There is often a lack of security and a threat of domestic violence. Some husbands may wreck the house or beat the wife up. Many men are afraid of letting their women out alone or of seeing them dress up to go somewhere by themselves. Sadly, too many of the men resort to violence to sort things out, whether with women, with their children or in disputes with other men. I guess that that is where the behaviour of leaders at the youth club can be an example to parents: we can show them you don't have to wallop kids in order to discipline them.

We tried to tackle 'identity' issues with some of the groups who met at The Bridge. We would ask: what does being a Protestant or a Loyalist mean? This was a difficult task. Many in the area never socialised outside it. You have to realise that a lot of working-class communities can be very isolated. Besides travelling to Spain for their summer holidays, they may never have had any real exposure to the outside world. The 'identity issue' surfaced most uncomfortably during the whole 'Drumcree' period. There were barricades just outside the centre. We turned the TV off in the café because it was causing people to get worked up during the news coverage of the protests.

I think that, all in all, we have made a difference to the local community over the years. We haven't had lots of 'converts' or planted new churches but we have positively redefined what Christianity is about for many people in the Ravenhill area. Doing this redefinition is all about changing the image of the church from that of being a kind of middle-class club. But am I optimistic about the future for the churches and the community in Northern Ireland? No I am not, for I see too many churches that are only interested in bigger programmes for their members and a bigger build. Where they do attempt community development, it is too often offering only skills and facilities for the few who will benefit from the help in order to move out of their community and away.

If churches do want to be positively involved with nearby communities they have to ask, above all, why they want to do it. They must be honest with themselves. They have to be prepared to offer themselves, their people and their premises without any immediate thought of payback. It's impossible to do too much groundwork. Observe the area you want to work in. Get to know it. Ask what is needed. Don't duplicate any effective Christian work already happening there and don't try to upstage it. Remember that you may benefit from the work you do as well as the people whom it is for. I was certainly blessed by experiences at The Bridge.

But remember that it's not just through doing the work on the ground that Christians can benefit deprived communities. Able Christians can lobby their local political representatives and think through the political issues involved in the government's decision-making. They can exercise a key role in arguing for a society where justice prevails.

Campbell Best, Youthworker, Co-ordinator of The Y Zone in Portadown

The Y Zone in Portadown has grown out of the Elim church, whose character is distinctly Pentecostal. This work operates in a mid-Ulster town that has been trying hard to shake off the sectarian image it had as the centre of the annual Drumcree standoff. Campbell Best is the current co-ordinator of the centre and his interview brings to light a whole other aspect to life in Portadown, involving the misuse of drugs and alcohol by young people, many of whom come from the Loyalist estates in the town. However, the problems with dysfunctional youth that Campbell's interview depicts in such stark detail are also to be found in other towns throughout Northern Ireland and indeed arguably in other postmodern urban environments in the western world, where traditional structures of community and family have broken down and young males, in particular, are vulnerable to all kinds of risk-taking, gang culture and addictive behaviour.

The Y Zone Drop-In Centre is located in a renovated part of the old Regal Cinema in Portadown town centre. It's an outreach project of the Portadown Elim Church. We have two full-time workers and 24 unpaid volunteers. Part of the funding comes from the church and part comes from businesses, statutory bodies, banks and charitable agencies. Eight years ago, I felt the need to target marginalised and at-risk kids, having already been involved in church-based youth work for some time. I had severe issues with alcohol in my own life before I became a born-again Christian, so I could identify with these youngsters.

In the past, we only really made contact with difficult and troubled young people when we engaged in occasional late-night outreach sessions. Now that the Y Zone exists, we work on a daily basis with these youngsters. My wife Gail and I had a passion to reach them and so that is how the work began. They gather on the Boulevard down by the River Bann, which is a notorious area for alcohol and drug abuse and crime. At first, we had some criticism from church people who wondered if there was any point in spending time with 'those drunk kids'. Now most local Christian and non-Christian people are very positive about our work.

At weekends, anything from 30 to 50 of them meet down there and several others meet at other locations close by. So numbers on the ground engaging in 'At Risk Behaviour' on any given night can be in excess of 250 young people. They drink cider, beer and alcopops and they take ecstasy, smoke cannabis and sometimes use solvents. There is a rise in availability of harder drugs such as cocaine. The vast majority of these young people are from the Loyalist estates in the town. Now that many of the paramilitary units who controlled the drug trade are being dismantled, there is an increased danger of young lads setting up their own drug-selling empires to make money and gain esteem. Some of the younger elements of these former paramilitary groups seem to be driving this new situation.

We regularly visit the Boulevard and some of the derelict spaces around Portadown, to find out what is going on. We have found socks, which the kids spray with deodorant so as to inhale the fumes. We have found canisters of Ronson lighter gas, which the kids also inhale. This is known as volatile substance abuse and one in four first-time users are vulnerable to a heart attack. That is why the police take a softly-softly approach rather than storming a place where they think that kind of abuse is going on. The shock could cause a young user to take a seizure and die.

Substances such as lighter fuel, deodorant, furniture polish and nail varnish are so readily available in the home and the parents will not easily detect that they are being used as a drug. Sadly, we had a young lad in the area who died from inhaling Lynx body spray. And we also had a 16-year old girl who died from this kind of substance abuse. We think that some of the 'graffiti artists' in the town are getting a 'double hit' by painting their graffiti but also sniffing the aerosol paint.

Underage drinking has got worse and the age at which it starts has fallen. It used to be that 13 or 14 was the age when they began but now it's 11 or 12. Why is this so? Well, in part because there are far more broken families. Twenty years ago, I would say that only 5% of the kids on the Boulevard came from a broken home. Now its 80-85%. Also, the attitudes to 'booze' have changed. This is partly due to the change in the licensing laws. There has been a massive moral shift and many of the youngsters we meet have started drinking at an early age in the presence of their families and that is considered acceptable. Many of these parents probably developed alcohol dependency during the Troubles in order to cope and they then tolerate alcohol use in their children. These children often run around town at all hours. We have seen 11-year olds who are out at three in the morning.

Our work is multifaceted. We sometimes have had to intervene when a young person who has been causing trouble is about to be 'given a lesson' by the paramilitaries. We often have to 'straddle' the needs of the young offender and the community in which he is wreaking havoc, by trying to help that young person but also to protect the people who are being harmed by his actions.

We have tried to show the Nationalist community in the town that we are friendly and willing to help them too. Our workers did a litter clean-up, wearing our Y Zone T-shirts, in parts of the town which have interface areas. Recently we have been able to host young Catholic lads here on the premises. It started when one of our workers intervened in an altercation in the town centre. He introduced himself to some of the Catholic boys and invited them to the Y Zone, which would hitherto have been considered a no-go area as the town has been a segregated space for over 30 years now, due to the conflict. A few came at first. Then one night many more arrived. We had tried carefully to prepare for their arrival so that it would be a safe environment for them, with a good staff/user ratio and someone posted in every room. The Protestant and Catholic lads have mixed remarkably well. There have been some tensions but we have seen them playing pool together and 'getting on'.

Now we have ethnic [minority] kids as well. Portuguese kids, Pakistanis, Romanians, Poles. I would say that now up to 5% of the local population is from a [minority] ethnic background. We have also had gay kids in the club. We try to treat them with real acceptance. It is only during one of our Christian talks that we might say something that hopefully gets them to think critically about aspects of the gay lifestyle that they are choosing and that Jesus can set them free.

We do allow football tops as we want young people to be able to express themselves. Staff only target negative, prejudicial attitudes when they occur. We operate from a clear Christian ethos. We are here to tell young people that life is a gift that God gave us and the greatest gift of all is that Christ died for them, regardless of their background or circumstances and that He desires that they surrender their lives to Him.

The Y Zone works in partnership with local community organisations such as Place Initiatives and various residents' associations as well as statutory bodies such as the Probation Board and the PSNI, the Southern Drugs and Alcohol team, the Northern Ireland Housing Executive, Craigavon Borough Council and the Southern Education and Library Board.

We believe that relationships are at the heart of everything. They are the genetic code of our work. We make connections. We allow ourselves to be vulnerable and to make mistakes, knowing we can overcome all difficulties through Christ. We try to show young people that God is interested in them. That they are 'beautifully and wonderfully made.' But so many of our youngsters are choosing a way that leads to death. It says in Numbers 16:48 that God is looking for people to stand between the living and the dead. To stand in the gap, in other words. We would see ourselves as standing in that gap.

And no matter where we are in life, we leave our personal lives behind when we come onto the premises to work with these kids. Our focus is totally on them. And we get rewards from time to time. We returned from a recent trip to America, during which we had had to temporarily close the premises. 'I really missed the smiling faces in the Y Zone' one girl said to us, when we came back 'Please don't close again...' I think that they all now feel considerable ownership of the centre. When some of our video games went missing, a lot of them chipped in together to replace the stolen goods. They now tend to challenge any new kid arriving at the club who breaks our rule about cursing or swearing on the premises. They expect discipline and we operate a yellow card and red card policy, like in football, for aggressive or inappropriate behaviour. If someone is behaving in a way that seriously endangers other youngsters then he is banned for life.

We try to create a Christian ambience. We play good, modern Christian music on CD or DVD. We leave relevant, accessible Christian literature lying around the place. They read it and ask us questions about our faith and our lifestyle. One commonly asked question is 'Why do you'se not drink?' and we explain how as Christians we just don't need to do that. All our workers have taken a pledge to abstain from alcohol. We are not concerned with the big general issue of whether Christians should or should not touch alcohol. We just know that we have to avoid compromising our values by drinking when we are working with the kind of young people we meet who are vulnerable to alcohol abuse. Our abstinence is a small personal sacrifice.

Regularly, we have short, relevant talks here at the Y Zone for schools or during drop-in evenings. Sometimes we have the 'Puppets of Praise' group doing puppet theatre with a Christian message or else we have a drama performance or a video. We try to cover what's relevant in young peoples' lives in order to positively impact on issues that may affect them.

We saw on our recent visit to the 'LA Dream Center' in California, how violent gang warfare is now so prevalent in youth culture all across the USA. It's heading our way and we only have to look at cities like London, Manchester and Birmingham to reinforce that reality. These new dangers will possibly replace the sectarian or paramilitary allegiances with which we have become familiar. But we at the Y Zone and the Elim church are here to stay, to invest in young peoples' lives, to build relationships, to communicate the relevance of the life of Jesus Christ and show his power to change a society in moral decline.

Remember what St Francis said. 'Go forth and preach the gospel at all times – and when necessary use words.'

Stephen Dallas, Project Officer for The Hard Gospel Project, based in Belfast

The Hard Gospel Project is an island-wide Church of Ireland initiative, which strives to combat sectarian and racist attitudes but also, among other things, to reconnect middle-class churches with working-classes citizens. One task in which full-time worker Stephen Dallas has been engaged may seem to the Evangelical mind to be a long way from the old-fashioned 'preaching of the gospel'. It may be perceived as an invaluable prelude to any meaningful Christian community engagement, although it is not to be seen just as an evangelistic 'warm-up act'. The 'Our Kind Of People' project is a faith-based attempt to build bridges and to foster much-needed self-esteem. It has been primarily undertaken in the Borough of Newtownabbey in County Antrim, centring on large council estates in Monkstown and Rathcoole.

The Hard Gospel Project is all about the biblical injunction to love God and your neighbour and so we have been engaged in celebrating the lives of some of the Loyalist working-class communities in which our churches are based.

I am currently involved in collecting 80 stories of people from Rathcoole. They are mostly individuals who have gone on to 'do something interesting' with their lives and the project is meant to give a sense of pride and achievement to local people in an estate where there is a lot of alienation and where young people often have very limited aspirations. I needed to recruit almost 50 volunteers to record these stories. Some of these helpers are church people and others are not. I have also had to set aside an evening to train them in how to conduct and record an interview.

I guess there is a bit of confusion both in churches and in the community about the nature of the project as nothing like this has been done before. I have found that there is a core of people in each congregation who really 'get it' and there are a lot of people who don't. I have also struggled to keep the project in the minds of the churches that have signed up to it. Of course, they have other things going on.

Each interview has to be written up and has to include who the person is, what their background in Rathcoole actually was, what they have been doing since they left school and then some sense of what their philosophy of life would be. A summary of the person is typed up and a photograph of them is taken. We make up posters, which include these biographical accounts and the photos. Then the posters are put together as an exhibition. We are calling this display the 'Our Kind Of People' exhibition and it will be placed in Rathcoole Youth Centre for one week.

I got the help of local churchgoers, local teachers and other community figures in order to locate a range of suitable subjects. Then I tried to pair off the interviewees and interviewers in positive ways, giving the famous footballer Jimmy Nicholl to some young people to talk to, for instance. I have then been able to get a community photographer from the 'Belfast Exposed' network to help with the photographic portraits. It has taken me five or six months to get the whole Rathcoole project running, through from initiation to completion. We have been fortunate to receive money to fund the work from the Department of Social Development's Local Community Fund, which has been administered through Newtownabbey Borough Council.

The work brings local churches together and gets them to reach out and engage. I discovered that the local congregations had never really worked on a joint project before! Now, in several other parts of Northern Ireland, there are people who want to copy what we have done. There is the possibility of a project in the Greater Shankill area, a cross-community one in Craigavon and another across the sectarian divide between Ballymacarrett and the Short Strand.

It is amazing the different things that Rathcoole people have gone on to do. There have been lots of sports people including a famous BBC Radio football commentator called Alan Green. There have also been plenty of pastors and ministers, including one who is now an Elim clergyman in Idaho! Then there are two local brothers who founded the Belfast Bus Company and became millionaires. However, it is important not to convey that an ordinary life simply spent in Rathcoole is some kind of failure. We should not talk down to a working-class community with a set of middle-class values. So I have also included many subjects who did not necessarily become famous or rich but just made a successful career out of an ordinary job. However, putting the more 'successful' Rathcoole people back in touch with their backgrounds was also a valuable way of connecting those who have moved away to their first community.

Could it one day be possible for the churches to do more of this kind of local history and eventually get Rathcoole to come to terms with some of the darker moments on the estate, during the 30 years of the Troubles? Perhaps there might be more hope of that kind of thing in other places. I don't think they are ready for that just yet in Rathcoole.

For church leaders, making contact with Loyalist paramilitaries during the days when they were on an official war-footing was always a tense and challenging ask, open to the accusation that as Christians these leaders were 'giving respectability' to the 'men of violence.' As earlier chapters have noted, such a 'them-and-us' moral stance has to be questioned, especially given the fact that many 'respectable' Protestant religious and political leaders were very happy to call on the 'hard men' when 'action' was needed, only to wash their hands of them when they were no longer required.

Now, in an era when the paramilitaries claim either to have 'stood down' or are about to do so, the attempt by churchmen and women to reach out to those who still live within a UDA or UVF culture may still be subject to disapproval. In spite of this, a number of Protestant clergy work hard to maintain a positive link with those who still possess status within paramilitary culture, or who once did, so as to keep bridges open to Loyalist communities.

Joe Fell, minister of Ebrington Presbyterian Church in Derry, who facilitated the discussion with a number of current and former UDA men already referred to in Chapter three, is one such. Although in no way connected to this or any other Christian institution, the men were comfortable sitting in the church premises talking about the issues faced by their community and their attitudes to faith. Also present were two UDA prisoners on day-release from gaol who were doing some painting and decorating work in the church buildings as a means of 'getting back into society'. The following interview provides further examples of efforts to maintain links.

Rev Mervyn Gibson, Westbourne Community Church, Lower Newtownards Road, Belfast

Mervyn Gibson is a Presbyterian minister who operates in the environment of inner-city East Belfast. Westbourne Community Church, situated on the Lower Newtownards Road, was often known, in bygone days, as the 'shipyard church', in an era when Harland and Wolff employed thousands of local men. In the wake of industrial decline, unemployment, poverty and low morale have been ongoing problems for the community, added to which has been widespread paramilitary membership in this strongly Loyalist district. Although his ministry has involved all the usual features of local church life, in this interview Mervyn was asked to describe the ways in which he has attempted to understand Loyalism as a whole and to interact with Loyalist paramilitaries in particular.

'The church has a lot of catching up to do, in order to connect to the Loyalist community. There has been an attempt to create a distance from Unionism and Loyalism, in reaction to an earlier era when the church and the Unionist establishment were allegedly hand in glove. There has also been a strong tendency 'not to let your hands get dirty' by building relationships with the paramilitaries. In my opinion you should relate to them – as indeed the church needs to relate to all elements within the community – it is the nature of the relationship that is the key. In respect of the paramilitaries, I would articulate my own relationship to them as being that of a 'critical friend'. I seek to encourage and enable pathways that move paramilitaries from unacceptable activities. These routes are by necessity more pragmatic than idealistic. One way is to integrate them into community life, alongside the churches, voluntary and statutory groups as joint stakeholders in fora of various kinds.

It seems to me that the community I know is a lot less oppressed by the paramilitaries now. There are less and less manifestations of paramilitary criminality e.g. loan sharking and there are

attempts to stop the demands for protection money from local businesses and building sites, where such activity existed. The change of atmosphere was illustrated to me two or three days after the most recent 12 July celebrations when I went into a local chip shop and I overheard two young fellows who would have been bandsmen talking to each other. They were discussing the fact that they were about to go out and play a game of football. When they did refer back to 'The Twelfth' they were chatting about girls they had met. A few years ago, they would have been far more pre-occupied with the violence at the local interface or the ban on a local Orange route.

I have often been a mediator between individuals, businesses, churches and the paramilitaries and between feuding paramilitary groups. For a simple example, I have gone directly to the leaders to get a stay of execution on a loan that can't be repaid. I have also officiated at various ceremonies where paramilitaries have been involved. I have also dedicated local Loyalist community murals such as the one in Willowfield, which commemorates the various battalions of the 36th Ulster Division in the Great War. I am happy to offer help when such ceremonies occur, providing they are community events. We have loaned chairs and equipment when an annual community service of remembrance occurs near our church, at a memorial to people who were murdered in the Troubles. Local community groups attend these events and the local community includes paramilitaries, thus they are present on many occasions.

In one sense, bringing Loyalist ex-combatants on board community development initiatives is relatively easy. They usually manifest discipline. They have had the toughening experience of gaol. They very often don't drink and usually have a strong sense of morals. Sometimes, churches are harder to get involved! And now that these paramilitaries are opting out of controlling their communities, the new danger is an increase in anti-social behaviour. Now that the police have minimum recruitment from working-class Protestants due to what I see as institutionalised discrimination, the PSNI don't have the same rapport or connectedness with those communities. In the attempt to win over new Republicans friends and be 'middle of the road' – legitimate and laudable aims in themselves – the police have, in fact, forgotten their 'old' friends or treat with contempt those from Loyalists communities.

No, it's not among the actual paramilitaries that there is the most difficulty in the Loyalist community. It's from an emerging generation that has no boundaries with regard to behaviour, no respect for self or anything else and no moral code or markers of any kind. The only way you get through to them is through relationships. You have to spend time with them and be patient and build their trust. And the trouble is that many of the church members see the church as a place that keeps them distinct from that kind of roughness. In a world where they had no means of 'getting on' and 'getting out' of their working-class communities, Christians often wanted to put a mark of progress between themselves and their neighbours, through belonging to a church and dressing up smartly to go to it every Sunday. Some do not like to see that barrier broken down.

The leaders of the churches in Northern Ireland should be doing more to equip their members for community involvement. I used to go to the Presbyterian College, to do a lecture to the students on community work from a Christian perspective, once a year. That is not enough. It has to be a core element to the curriculum if we are serious about being salt and light and building relationships – if we are serious about the whole gospel. How does a cleric learn to reach out? How does he release his congregation to do it? Urban ministry is changing all the time. There are lots of young professionals moving into the new apartments in the inner city. We have never looked at this issue in the church! And there are lots of migrants in the inner city now too. I must say that I do not particularly know how to help them with their needs.

You can find yourself juggling lots of different roles as a minister. You can end up being 'used' to do different tasks for the community. However, you will often see some fruit in two or three years' time. I have had paramilitaries whom I worked with in the past phone me up and say 'Pray for me' or 'Please visit my granny in hospital…' You have to do everything with unconditional love.

Rev Robert Miller, Maghera Church of Ireland, County Londonderry

Robert Miller, the Church of Ireland rector in Maghera, County Londonderry, is another minister who has attempted to build genuine links with Loyalism of all shades, in this case in order to help a rural Protestant community that feels itself to be a beleaguered minority within a Republican environment in South County Londonderry. For Robert, the link with Orangeism has been the big challenge – particularly in regard to the issue of contentious parades.

I began as a curate with Rev Ken Good in Shankill Parish in Lurgan. That's where I got the experience of working with a team and of seeing the gospel not just as a message to be proclaimed but as something to be lived out in a caring ministry. The Orangeism there was really quite bitter and defensive. There were huge demographic changes in the area, involving Protestants moving out of parts of the town that they had lived in for years. Drumcree was also happening not far away at Portadown. During Ken's time the select vestry tried to challenge the political ethos of the church, including the flying of Loyalist and Union flags from the church tower.

After that I moved to Tullylish, a rural parish near Banbridge. People felt less threatened there. The Orangeism was different. It was more possible to encourage members to reach out the hand to local Roman Catholics. Four years ago, I came to Maghera, which is very different again. We have 320 families in the parish and I am also responsible for the church at Swattragh, which has a much smaller congregation. There is a general sense in this vicinity that the Protestant population is diminishing.

I have made an attempt to engage with all community groups in the area, including those which represent Orangeism and the various other shades of Loyalism as well as those who belong to the Nationalist and Republican camp, who are very much in the majority in South Derry. Orangeism here tends to emphasise the religious rather than the political side of the order. I have come to the conclusion that the Church of Ireland is in serious danger of just washing its hands of the Loyal Orders. For too long, Loyalists have felt that the church disapproves of them. This seems unfortunate, especially when a high percentage of the church members here are in a lodge.

There is opposition from Nationalists to the route the local Orangemen take on the morning of the Twelfth of July. There is also concern about the arrival into a largely Republican town of a crowd of Loyalist bandsmen from other areas in the North during an annual band contest that occurs in the town. To help with the parades issue and any other similar problems, we have set up a Forum for Accountable Community Engagement, which is affiliated to the Maghera Parish Caring

Association and is ready to talk to anyone in order to help resolve disputes. The late Billy Mitchell came from Belfast and was supported by Tony Macaulay in the setting up of the Forum. We employ a part-time worker, who is also fulfilling a function as our youth officer, part-time, to provide him with full-time hours.

In my experience, although you must get close to members of the Loyal Orders as a minister and you should help them to think through and articulate their position, you mustn't end up as their chaplain. You must not be simply 'a voice for your community' but also a critical presence. I work with the local Elim pastor and we try to be honest brokers between the bands and marchers and the local residents groups, which are mostly Nationalist or Republican-led. We will listen to all the parties and we don't rant at anyone. We also use trained mediators to help when tensions become heightened, although I have now done some training myself in mediation. It is important that we do this work rather than join the exit of clergymen from Northern Ireland during the 'marching season'.

In 2006, there were heightened community tensions when the Parades Commission awarded the local lodge the right to march to the top of the town on the Twelfth of July. This was a 'traditional route' but had been banned in recent years, as this is now a dominantly Republican part of town. The Order had originally requested the right to the reinstatement of this route but now they realised that if they went ahead there would be serious conflict on the streets of the town due to a mass protest by the local 'Concerned Residents Group'. In the end, we negotiated a situation where the lodges did not parade to the top of the town after all and any Nationalist protests were called off. The local lodges' feeder parade in 2007 initially applied for the top of the town, but subsequently for the benefit of lowering tensions in the local community walked the shortened route of 2006.

In 2008, we will have to do more mediation, possibly involving up to 40 meetings, as the County Londonderry 12th July parade will be held in Maghera and a lot of bands and Orangemen will be here. If that goes 'belly up' then the traditional annual band contest in Maghera, later in the summer, will also be in danger of becoming a source of community conflict. We will be talking to all the relevant parties from the local Loyalist and Republican community leaders to the local elected representatives. There have been other negotiations in the last few years, including trying to stop an inflammatory sectarian graffiti campaign from escalating into physical violence.

You are constantly walking a tightrope in this kind of work. However the Elim pastor and I seem to have built up a good relationship with most parties including the local Orangemen and indeed we have gone down to the Orange Hall and prayed with them on the morning of the Twelfth of July, before they set off for the day's march for the last three years. This met with a positive reaction. I am also glad to have good backing from my bishop and it is important to keep him informed of all that I am doing. I also liaise with my select vestry. However there is still an entrenched sectarianism in many quarters and it is especially disturbing when you see it in the young. It is also important to remember that a lot of security force members were killed in this area and that almost everyone had someone close to them – whether a friend, relative or neighbour – who was murdered over the years. This created a slow but very real traumatisation of the whole Protestant community which takes years to heal.

Councillor Dr John Kyle, Progressive Unionist Party, Pottinger Ward, East Belfast

John Kyle is an instance of a Christian from a professional background who has chosen to identify himself with left-of-centre party politics within the Protestant working-class heartland of East Belfast. His vehicle of choice is the Progressive Unionist Party, which sprang out of the militant Ulster Volunteer Force and has always struggled to achieve political influence, given the dominance in most working-class Loyalist communities of the Democratic Unionists, once headed by Ian Paisley.

As a Christian student at Queen's University in Belfast, I had the experience of being baptised in the Holy Spirit. Eventually I found myself involved in the Community of the King, enjoying a house-church based spirituality that was attempting to be truly cross-community. I then moved to London and was heavily committed to the Antioch Community, part of an international network known as the 'Sword of the Spirit' group, combining my work as a GP with my role as a part-time pastor. I spent seven years in London and it was a seminal time for me, in which I learnt about the post-Christian social context, which exists in most of Western Europe, and experienced the greater liberty of expression which can be enjoyed outside of the constraints of Northern Ireland's 'Christian' culture.

Moving back to the North in 1993, I joined the Christian Community Church in Belfast and our primary concern in these years seemed to be to further bridge the gap between the two communities through all kinds of joint worship events and conferences. We then began to ask politicians from every kind of political party to talk to us. We also invited representatives from a variety of community groups. We were trying to do 'applied Christianity', if you like.

Then, in the period of the 'Good Friday' Agreement, I was particularly struck by the emergence on the scene of the Progressive Unionist Party, fronted by Billy Hutchinson and David Ervine. Their kind of Unionism seemed to be positive, working class and conciliatory. Somehow, it resonated with my own spirituality. While 'cross-community' work had been extensively carried out by many Christians, I had a sense that the churches had not really connected with the Protestant working-class communities on their own doorsteps, which was a pity because people really seemed to have suffered through the years of the conflict.

My wife had become deeply involved in health promotion issues and she alerted my attention to the ways in which ill-health in working-class areas was caused by the whole social, cultural and economic environment. There were poor jobs or no jobs at all. There were poor educational prospects. There was cramped housing and there were streets strewn in glass or back alleyways covered in graffiti and full of litter. People turned to cigarettes and alcohol, which worsened their health and depleted their finances. I began to see that, despite the pietism of my earliest faith experiences, there was a need to work out the gospel in terms of community involvement, social justice and a Christian response to poverty. The faith that I had grown up with tended to emphasise Mary's role as opposed to Martha's! It often expressed itself in devotional rather than active Christianity. Perhaps those Catholic writers were right who spoke of all of life as a sacrament. I decided to become active, to get involved in politics, so I joined the Pottinger Branch of the Progressive Unionist Party.

At first I don't know what they made of Dugald McCullough and myself. We were the only two middle-class people in the party, or so it seemed. I went along to party conferences and spoke in debates. Then I was elected chairman of the local branch. I was nominated as deputy chairman of the party, which meant I was on the executive. Tragically, David Ervine died in January 2007 and whilst Dawn Purvis took over his role as a PUP MLA at Stormont, I was asked to stand for David's seat on the Council. I felt very honoured to do so and I reduced my hours in the surgery so as to leave one day a week to devote properly to Council business. I find it a very fulfilling task to be a councillor. I feel I am a voice for the more disadvantaged and more vulnerable in the city.

What about the party's links with the Ulster Volunteer Force? I am convinced that the paramilitaries have moved on from violence. And there is a certain pride which party members feel, realising that they made the successful transition from armed conflict to democratic politics. It's a triumph for the power of change. And the truth is that despite the violence in which many of them engaged, the men of the UVF were also capable of progressive political thinking. You see, the media is all too keen to portray the average Loyalist as a thug, with his knuckles scraping the ground and his arms covered in sectarian tattoos. Middle-class Protestants are particularly dismissive. They forget that many Loyalist working-class communities have had it very tough in a way that they themselves have not.

No, if, as a Christian, you want to change things, then you have to get in there and be involved with the way actually things are, instead of waiting around until it's 'safe' or respectable to do so. Jesus associated with all kinds of people and so can we. As for the party members' perception of me, they all know that my work springs from my Christian convictions. But of course, when I am doing my Council work, I am not in church; I am doing politics, which is different.

The deprivation is very real in places like the Lower Newtownards Road. Those who receive benefits may have enough to survive but they have very little safety margin. Often they can't afford to buy 'healthy food' – organic is an unaffordable luxury. There are few opportunities for improving your lot. A lad who goes to Belfast Metropolitan College to learn a trade will be asked to find a work placement for himself. He just doesn't know how to undertake that task. He doesn't know anyone who owns a business and wouldn't have the confidence to approach them, even if he did. So he leaves the course. That is the way kids end up perpetuating a culture of joblessness.

The educational system here reinforces a sense of low self-esteem. Inner-city kids are labelled a failure at an early age. There are few expectations of success and few good role models. The problem in this area can be as much emotional as financial poverty. The bad environment reinforces the sense of unhappiness. And Protestants who have 'moved on' are very bad at 'giving back' to their own communities. They should try harder to 'get behind' their culture. Even if they have 'moved out' to a nice house in Gilnahirk, they can still channel their skills back into a community like this, offering some of their abilities to help regenerate the area.

We need to see more pride in what it means be an East Belfast Protestant. It's not just about marching bands and Scottish dancing, it's about producing creative people like Van Morrison and Pete Wilson and it's about storytelling – confidently telling the story of our own lives and the life of our community.

Pastor Alan Hoey, Monkstown Baptist Church,Newtownabbey, County Antrim

Pastor Alan Hoey works as leader of the Monkstown Baptist Church in Newtownabbey in County Antrim. His attitude to the militant Loyalists who are the dominant force in the local council estate is forthright and clear. He would appear to be respected for the stand which he takes on the need for a personal experience of salvation and for the changes in morals and lifestyle that are needed when an individual embraces the Christian message. The Monkstown church is clearly attempting to relate in meaningful ways to a community that has been saturated by paramiltarism for decades.

Our church strives to reach out to the Loyalist Monkstown estate, which has a population of almost two and a half thousand, although it used to have many more. I guess that my own background helped me to empathise with Loyalist people, in the work I was about to do. My own father was in the Loyalist Vanguard movement in the 1970s.

When I first came to Monkstown as a pastor, there was a chap called Gordon Campbell in the congregation who had been a UVF man before his conversion and who had been motivated to go around UVF homes and into the UVF club to try and reach paramilitaries and their families with the gospel. He got rebuffed quite a lot but when I arrived I decided to join Gordon on his visits and because I was there as the local pastor, they seemed to accept us both more. In particular, we seemed to strike up a relationship with Billy Greer, a key local UVF figure. I explained my position – that I regarded the men in the club as lost souls in need of a Saviour. He seemed to accept that and said we would be welcome at any time. I was reminded of that verse from Revelations 3 'I have set before thee an open door that no man can shut…'

It is easy for people in a community like the Monkstown estate who have become Christians to move up and get out, economically and socially, because they are probably no longer wasting several hundred pounds a month on cigarettes and alcohol. However the danger then is that a 'local church', close to that estate, is no longer local. We are trying to avoid losing touch with local people. We do have many members who drive in from elsewhere but we have several church members who live on the estate. We want to be a church that is not hedged in. A church that is trying hard, even though that may mean making mistakes. We have to build bridges to the people and we have to be there as a moral centre in a society that is, in so many ways, falling apart.

We run family 'fun days' in the estate once a year and there's tea and buns for the adults, hot dogs for the kids and football coaching and a bouncy castle to provide entertainment. But our evangelistic ethos is still prominent – in recent years we got permission to erect a tent next to the UVF club and held a mission. The place was 'bunged' every night with UVF members and their wives. The leadership asked us could we do both the 'fun day' and the mission every year! The church choir has even gone into the club to sing. We have also taken the local kids to Whitehead for the day, to do sports. It was a huge success and much appreciated.

Recently, I was asked to take Billy Greer's funeral when he died. We had 1,000 people present and there was a real sense of reverence throughout. There was just a guard of honour made up of the committee of the Friends of the Somme, of which he was a member. A lone piper played hymns. Not long before, I had been presenting Bibles to the estate's football committee and I made a point of giving Billy one with his name written on it in special calligraphy. He was almost in tears when he saw it. 'You have made my day' he said to me. 'Will you read it?' I asked. 'Ah, sure you know me…' he replied but then he hinted that he would. I just hope that he did. A few weeks later he was dead.

What worries me is that as the old paramilitary structure dissolves, pure gangsterism will take its place. We have to be in there as a church with a moral voice, trying to prevent that from happening. We have to be up-front about who we are and what we believe. I believe that people in Monkstown respect that and even those who disagree with us are prepared to be courteous. There is a vast amount to do and we must try to win the estate for Christ, one step and one family at a time. This may mean stepping out of our traditional ways of thinking about church.

For example, we need to create a powerful sense of Christian community. If a UVF man becomes a Christian and no longer wants to go to the club every night as he used to do, what is there for him, within the church, to replace that intense sense of community? I am glad that many of the younger people in our church can see that we need to respond to this need, so that it is more and more of a Christian community that embraces its members, instead of a club which is there just to be attended every weekend.

As will have been clear from the interviews contained in this chapter, Christian community work comes in various shapes and guises, involves a range of skills and presents a daunting set of challenges. For anyone wishing to make a start on a Christian community project, sound advice is crucial and a sense of collegiality invaluable. Help may be found within denominational structures and from other bodies, such as the Churches and Community Work Alliance, which possess a wealth of expertise. Tearfund's 'Church Community and Change' programme provides the structure and support to enable churches to respond to the needs of their local communities as part of a facilitated process which can take between nine and eighteen months. The organisation Community Work from a Christian Perspective offers a forum in which to share problems and strategies with fellow-practitioners.

This book has outlined some of the basic social, historical and cultural knowledge required for anyone contemplating greater community involvement, but hopefully it will also have provided a little bit of inspiration from hearing others recount their own journeys towards meaningful engagement.

[1] The interviewees who have not been named met with the author under conditions of anonymity. Most of the interviews in this chapter are, however, denoted by name, role and location. All interviews took place during the latter half of 2007. Some of the information contained in this chapter was obtained during visits to the work in question, rather than relying on an interview.

conclusion

This survey has looked at the deprivation and despair that characterises too many Protestant working-class communities. It has assessed the nature of the Loyalism that pervades these communities and it has caught a glimpse of the church's recent relationship with Loyalists – or, in many cases, the lack of it. A chapter has also been devoted to relevant social problems and Christian ministry elsewhere in the world. Other chapters have looked at the contribution of recent faith-based community work in Northern Ireland and in particular at the legacy of Billy Mitchell – stressing both his practical contribution and his seminal Christian thinking.

It should be clear from this survey that the Protestant church in working-class communities has often foundered. It needs to put a positive relationship in place by offering its very considerable resources and skills for the good of those communities as well as vocally proclaiming its age-old message of spiritual rebirth. However it should be apparent that the church also needs to do some thinking. It must take up the combative challenge of analysing what has gone wrong in Northern Irish society in the light of gospel values. It must suggest or model alternatives. This involves 'getting down and dirty' in tough areas of economic policy and political decision-making. In the case of the Loyalist communities that we have studied, it involves thinking about ideology – asking questions about how a blind faith in a particular template of 'Britishness' has not helped working-class communities out of a place that lacks expectation, well-being and hope.

It should be apparent in this book that the legacy of the Troubles is about much more than the lost lives and bereaved families who are its most tragic consequence. A lot of people in Loyalist communities are still trapped and troubled, economically and culturally, while middle-class Protestants have been able to adapt to change, 'move on' and in very many cases thrive. However for Christians to make an attempt to 're-neighbour' these communities may well be a revolutionary business, involving what Bob Lupton calls 'downward mobility'. It may thus involve sacrifice – but then should being a follower of Christ in post-Troubles Northern Ireland consist of anything less?

A multi-cultural challenge may lie ahead for this society. It is easy to accept immigration as an enrichment process if you are in a position of economic and social comfort. For Loyalist communities, there are not many such comfort zones. To them a multi-cultural future often looks frightening and unjust. The church's embrace of racial tolerance must be rooted in an understanding of how a multi-cultural society looks from the point of view of a working-class man or woman who lives on the margins of society, both in terms of economic struggle and political disempowerment.

Christian thinkers in this part of Ireland, as elsewhere in the world, must develop new theological insights, based on the experience of fighting for the rights of – and attempting to re-animate – broken, conflicted and impoverished communities. After all, if current demographic trends are anything to go by, the majority of the world's population will soon be living in gigantic cities, often characterised by wealth for the few and degradation for the many. Theology as mere speculation about God and his ways, in the lecture rooms of academia, undertaken on behalf of affluent Western churches, must be seen as deeply limited.

To that end, a new, innovative ecclesiology for 'doing church' in Loyalist communities in post-Troubles Northern Ireland needs to emerge. Copying the regimes utilised in the 'chilled-out' lifestyle-oriented mega-churches of the sunshine states in the USA is surely the wrong policy. The distance from Silicon

Valley to Ballybeen is too great.

The church forms that do emerge will be rooted in a clear-sighted, compassionate interaction with the human need and the communal alienation that Christ himself once witnessed in a troubled and oppressed backwater of the Roman Empire. These forms will also allow for celebration of the enduring courage and robust dignity that can characterise working-class culture and for the retention of those values in the Loyalist heritage that are life-enhancing.

Need and alienation are ultimately rooted in the habit humans have of turning away from God – a phenomenon which the Bible calls sin. However, social structures are usually devised by those who do not have God-centredness as their core value and so they too can be a formidable expression of sin. Social structures may thus need changed by the power of the gospel as well as human hearts, if the battle with sin is to be undertaken.

Finally, in light of the powerful theological lessons learned in Billy Mitchell's Long Kesh prison cell, this survey calls for seminary education to be changed so that an intense acquaintance with the human condition is placed at the very core of the learning process undertaken by church leaders. Ideally, at least a year spent by trainees in 'coal-face' community work would be the necessary prelude to almost any serious theological study whatsoever. This would be a considerable help if the church of tomorrow is to learn a set of new loyalties to the struggling communities whose plight has been the motivation for this study.

Acknowledgements

New Loyalties represents an innovative and timely exploration of the relationship between Protestant Churches and Protestant working class communities. It also represents a collaborative project that has brought together a disparate group of organisations and individuals in a sincere attempt to build bridges of understanding and active engagement.

I would therefore like to thank all those who made this work possible and to name a few in particular for their unique contribution.

Anna Rankin for her editorial skills and good sense of humour. Michelle McFadden for her scrutiny and proofreading. Merve Jones of Spring Graphics for his design and layout and also his well considered photography. Michael Bradley for his background research and willingness to do just about anything. Dorothy Monahan, from the IFI Community Bridges Programme, for her patient support and understanding. And of course to Phillip Orr for his tenacious commitment to this project and his ability to write with accuracy and inspiration.

In particular I want to thank the many men and women whose community and church based projects provide the best insight and practical learning in the resource. For their love of life and commitment to people we are grateful.

Derek Poole
Project Co-ordinator.

Philip Orr is a writer and researcher living in Carrickfergus, Co Antrim. His most frequent topic has been the Great War in Irish history. His publications include, *Field of Bones - an Irish Division at Gallipoli* (2006), *Tom's Story - Sentry Hill and the Great War* (2007) and *The Road to the Somme* (1987, 2008). He is a member of Fitzroy Presbyterian Church, Belfast.